CREATION, SIN, COVENANT, AND SALVATION

Creation, Sin, Covenant, and Salvation: A Primer for Biblical Theology

‿

EDWARD P. MEADORS

CASCADE *Books* · Eugene, Oregon

CREATION, SIN, COVENANT, AND SALVATION
A Primer for Biblical Theology

Cascade Books
An Imprint of Wipf and Stock Publishers
199 W. 8th Ave., Suite 3
Eugene, OR 97401

www.wipfandstock.com

ISBN 13: 978-1-61097-072-3

Cataloging-in-Publication data:

Meadors, Edward P.

Creation, sin, covenant, and salvation : a primer for biblical theology / Edward P.
Meadors.

xiv + 126 p. ; 23 cm. Includes bibliographical references.

ISBN 13: 978-1-61097-072-3

1. Covenant theology—Biblical teaching. 2. Creation—Biblical teaching. 3. Sin—
Biblical teaching. 4. Atonement. 5. Bible—Evidences, authority, etc. I. Title.

BS1199.C6 M46 2011

Manufactured in the U.S.A.

This book is dedicated to the administration, faculty, and staff of Taylor University.

All author royalties from the sales of this book will be donated to the Taylor Fund, which provides financial aid to worthy students of need.

"these things have been written that you may believe that Jesus is the Christ, the Son of God; and that believing you may have life in his name."

(John 20:31)

"from childhood you have known the sacred writings which are able to give you the wisdom that leads to salvation through faith which is in Christ Jesus."

(2 Tim 3:15)

Contents

Preface ix

1. Eden: Fact or Fairy Tale? 1

2. It's a Humpty Dumpty World: Sin and its Consequences 28

3. The Covenant Solution: It's All About Relationships 51

4. Salvation: What God Made, He can Fix 77

5. The Self-Authenticating Power of Scripture 105

Bibliography 125

Preface

Creation, Sin, Covenant, and Salvation is a primer in biblical theology that is accessible to lay readers of all ages. Sprinkled with anecdotes and illustrations, the book eases readers into theological discussion of the four interrelated topics that constitute the title—creation, sin, covenant, and salvation. The book closes with a final chapter that explains the authority, practical value, and intended purpose of Scripture. While not intimidating, the book challenges readers to think critically about the real life believability of the Christian faith, especially its intellectual coherence.

The understanding of the Bible as "able to give the wisdom that leads to salvation through faith in Jesus Christ" (2 Tim 3:15) is a control and corrective throughout, as the author explains why the Scriptures were written, how they interrelate, and for what ultimate purpose. In keeping with biblical theology, the book affirms the continuity of biblical revelation as it climaxes in God's consummation of his original creative plan.

After finishing *Creation, Sin, Covenant, and Salvation*, readers will:

- Understand the wisdom of "all Scripture" that leads to salvation in Jesus Christ.

- Understand how the Bible's many parts interrelate to tell the epic story of God's revelation in Scripture.

- Encounter relevant topics for the contemporary world including the Bible's stance toward pop culture, pornography, movies, video games, marriage, pluralism, and the exclusivity of the Christian faith.

- Gain an understanding of how scriptural truth relates to comprehensive reality.

- Gain a better understanding of why some people reject the Christian faith.

Experience has taught me that the instruction of *Creation, Sin, Covenant, and Salvation* is accessible and enlightening to high school youth groups, college students, and Christian adults. While theological tomes are impressive collectibles for the shelf, what most Christians today need is a short readable primer that explains the thought world of the Bible in comprehensible terms.

I have discovered that many Christians today are intimidated by theological sophistication. Technical terms, references to Greek and Hebrew, and foreign ancient cultures make what began as a personal encounter with God into a sophisticated intellectual headache. This intimidation is unfortunate and not necessary. In truth, biblical theology is simple and related to the everyday realities of our contemporary world. The most important truths of Scripture are accessible to us all. We only have to see them to understand.

I have also discovered that there is a disconnect in the minds of many Christians between faith and reality. Reality is the world of science and cold hard fact. Faith is the world of religion, mystical experience, and cultural tradition. Like separate compartments, both serve their purposes—the one practical, the other spiritual.

The casualty of this disconnect, however, is the truth of reality where authentic objects of faith are real—creation really does exist; sin is a reality that has real destructive consequences; responsible loving relationships are really possible in our fractured world; forgiveness really works, and, yes, reconciliation after sin can really happen.

Similarly, as simple and sloppy science has undesirable consequences, so too does irresponsible and thoughtless theology. To get biblical theology wrong is to get *reality* wrong—to live with a faulty, contorted worldview. Understanding of scriptural truth is understanding of real truth that aids human beings in understanding reality as it really is. It's the distortion of Scripture that disturbs intelligent people.

Chapter by chapter, *Creation, Sin, Covenant, and Salvation* prompts the reader to consider the reality of biblical revelation in our contemporary world. Intellectually, I'm convinced that Christianity is coherent, rational, and fully compatible with all of reality as we know it. The world is just what we would expect it to be based on Scripture. Belief is not a pipe dream; it's an understanding of things as they really are.

But that's my frank opinion. Readers are encouraged to read with critical minds and discriminating judgment to reach their own conclusions about God. A belief that results from persuasion or indoctrination is neither authentic nor stable. Such is the imposter that so often misrepresents authentic Christian faith.

The goal of *Creation, Sin, Covenant, and Salvation* is the understanding of true Christianity as revealed in Scripture. We will discover that if we appraise God for who he reveals himself to be, he far exceeds human limitations and what we would find naturally believable—if God were a human being. But Scripture does not call us to believe in God as another human being. Humanity is not the benchmark for God. It's God's infinite superiority that defines God as God and makes believable the humanly impossible. In this thought world, miracles are not magic but things God can do that human beings can't. The Creator can control creation in ways that created beings can't.

To this awareness, the Bible takes us. God's truth makes sense of our reality, but his reality extends far beyond. *Creation, Sin, Covenant, and Salvation* prompts readers to consider not only the realities of sin but also the greater and more powerful realities of God's re-creative power, which explains the realities of joy and eternal hope amidst the degenerating realities of physical deterioration and death. God's re-creative power is a higher dimension of reality that does more than pacify the fears of the human heart. It inspires the confident peace that God's creative love will defeat evil at its hellish worst and restore abundant life in a new heavens, a new earth, and a people composed of resurrected, newly created bodies. No, it's not a pipedream. If God is God, it's reality—if he loves us and chooses to exercise his creative power once more in our behalf.

But that "if" is a barrier that many today find insurmountable. Many, of course, have eyes but cannot see God and have minds but cannot comprehend him. Are you such a person? If so, I would encourage you to think about the God of biblical revelation before you reject his existence. Perhaps the god you reject isn't God at all but only his misrepresentation. Perhaps what you reject is the god of your tradition, the god of your culture, the god of someone else's imagination, or the prefabricated "straw god" of a misinformed influence—someone reacting to the disillusion of their own false god or false Christianity. If that's the case, you are wise to reject the gods and Christianities you don't believe in.

But don't give up on God prematurely. Agnostic and atheistic rejections of God are expectations of biblical revelation. The Bible leads us to expect intellectual cynicism. For such is the expected countenance of those who consider God not worth thinking about (Rom 1:28), who readily endorse the cynic's spin, who refuse to genuinely call upon God in prayer, who stand aloof from genuine communion with the people of God, who disassociate from God when it's to their professional advantage, and who detach themselves from devotion to God in times of intellectual, emotional, or relational challenge. If people choose to go their own way, God allows them to do so.

According to the Bible, God has given human beings over to the freedoms of their own devices (Rom 1:18–32). If people do not want God, he does not violate their wills. If people do not want relationship with God, God does not force himself upon them (Rev 3:20). If people don't want to think about God, they are free to discover the consequences of life apart from him. Such is the reality of the mortal world we live in. God is not a Juggernaut; he doesn't desire blind devotion. He desires true worship from the heart in spirit *and* truth. He desires intimate relationship characterized by faith, forgiveness, relational faithfulness, responsible love, and eternal commitment. Salvation is a relationship, not a command or imposition.

According to the Bible, God is an infinitely superior being, but his sovereignty is not impersonal. To the contrary, his sovereignty perfects the virtues of justice, mercy, grace, forgiveness, purity, faithfulness, patience, holiness, compassion, and sacrificial love. These truths are a problem for the atheist. From where do they come? . . . the evolution of unthinking, unfeeling inanimate matter? Is that conjecture really persuasive?

We can't say these truths don't exist, because we innately sense their reality and we order our world around them. We have emotions. We have judicial systems. We have poetry. We have music. We have art. We laugh. We cry. We mourn. We grieve. We rejoice. We imagine. We love. We give sacrificially to those in need.

These truths take us beyond the explanations of secular Darwinism. Survival of the fittest logic has no explanation for sacrificial agape love. Darwinism may explain the Holocaust, but it doesn't have an answer for the cross. The cross is a problem.

Wanting to be known, God has created a world that bears his fingerprints. Thus he has revealed within Scripture his true character—a character of supreme love that desires reconciliation and atonement. According to the Bible, if you search for him, you will find him, and when you find him, you will not be disappointed (Deut 4:29; Rom 9:33). You will find fulfillment and satisfaction where it can actually be found—not in competitive self-promotion, but in things of eternal value—in responsible relationship with the human family, pleasure in God's creation, pleasure in doing God's work, and in eternal intimate relationship with God himself. Considering the stakes, why not look into the matter with seeing eyes and an open mind?

1

Eden: Fact or Fairy Tale?

Do you understand the Bible? Do you understand how the Bible's many parts interrelate to tell the epic story of God's revelation in Scripture? Can you go beyond facts, figures, dates, memory verses, lists, and scholarly words to express the Bible's comprehensive message? Do you really know the wisdom of "all Scripture" that leads to salvation in Jesus Christ? Can you articulate why the Bible is a trustworthy guide for living in our multifaceted contemporary world? Is your understanding of the Bible really yours, or is it what you've inherited with conviction and passion but never really thought through in depth on your own?

These big questions cannot be answered in a class, a degree, or in a flashy monograph. Biblical theology is a journey of daily thought that spans one's entire lifetime. It involves daily meditation over Scripture attended by prayer and worship in the body of Christ, the church. It involves conversation with the thoughts of other theologians, past and present, celebrated and obscure, as well as modest lay persons who genuinely desire knowledge of the truth.

Biblical theology seeks to understand reality as it is revealed in the Bible from Genesis to Revelation. Working from the awareness that the Bible reveals a diverse yet coherent message, biblical theology confronts the contemporary world with a radical and countercultural worldview—that God really does exist, that he created us, loves us, has a design for how we should live, wants to rescue us, and will in the end determine our eternal fate. Biblical theology is about God's kingship, his plan, and his work within history and within humanity to achieve his ultimate end. Biblical theology is a coherent story and a worldview.

Biblical theology is also evangelical. It professes to be the truth and to be good news to those who receive it in obedient, active faith, and as a result are transformed by the renewing of their minds. God's goodness surpasses the capacity of words as he defeats evil with good right up to the creation of the resurrected body and the new heavens and the new earth. His glory has no end. Nothing is impossible with God.

This little book may be rightly categorized as a primer—a primer on biblical theology. Like a primer on a small gasoline engine, it is my hope that these pages will successfully ignite thoughts and conversations that will lead to productive reading of Scripture and a deeper understanding of God's story and humanity's place within it. Functioning as a primer, we will discuss the contemporary relevance of Scripture in non-academic terms and incorporate illustrations and anecdotes here and there to keep the engine going. However, creation, sin, covenant, and salvation will remain our constant focus as they are the vital organs of Scripture—overlapping themes essential to an understanding of every book of the Bible. It all begins with God and his creation of reality.

Surprised by Reality

Kathy and I had no business being there. But I was a struggling young professor, and the prospect of an affordable vacation was irresistible. So two days before, we loaded up the kids for an all expenses paid vacation in Beckley, West Virginia—a luxurious holiday in exchange for enduring a sales pitch for a "once in a lifetime investment opportunity."

In truth the sales pitch was not nearly the hard sell that I'd suffered the summer before in Branson, Missouri, or the summer before that in Crossville, Tennessee. There was no arm-twisting or seductive coercion, just a short painless presentation. When that was over and my VISA card and bank account were secure from danger, I felt tremendous relief—like I'd slipped through customs unnoticed or dodged a speeding ticket with a mere reprimand. Out of harm's way, I breathed deeply and settled into full vacation mode.

Moments later the tires of our minivan came to a grumbling halt at the majestic mountain property that "could be ours." Meandering about, we found an opening in the forest and began a descent into the wooded darkness. What followed has been with me ever since.

No, this was not the stuff of a blockbuster hit. We didn't stumble upon a violent crime scene with bloodied, dismembered body parts. We were not attacked by an escaped criminal. We didn't discover a hidden stash of Confederate gold. Nor did we chance upon a celebrity, see a UFO, or have an encounter with an angel. Instead we found ourselves in the middle of a mountainous expanse that had never been disturbed—ever. Fingerprints of humankind were entirely absent. No bottle tops, no plastic grocery bags, no cigarette butts, no rusty machine parts from yesteryear. We were in a virgin forest of mature hardwoods, blooming Mountain Laurels, and gigantic lichen spotted boulders.

Scurrying up a massive rock, I was intoxicated by the life surrounding me. My vocabulary proved totally inadequate with the worn out cliché *"unbelievable"* being all that I could muster. The absence of a thesaurus at the depths of my innermost being was humbling. But that was ok. Exaggerations elsewhere were here fitting and true. The pure beauty of that moment was, in truth, unbelievable. It was awesome. We were in a cathedral of intoxicating life, a sanctuary of the purest kind. In all my travels, real or imaginary, I'd never experienced anything like it.

Most amazing to me was the fact that this place was real. And as the reality of the moment sank in, so did the truth of a childhood fairy tale. As I gazed upward at the forest canopy, reality suddenly surpassed the fanciful. "This is like the garden of Eden," I whispered. *And it was.*

To write further in memory of this event would require poetry. And I am most definitely not a poet—at least not a good one. Nor do I want to give the impression that I'm in the mold of Henry David Thoreau or John Denver—both of whose talents far exceed my own. Yet, despite my average aesthetic aptitude, I left that forest invigorated, inspired, and with a vivid memory of a reality that bordered on the fantastic. I would love to go back.

We thought seriously about a mortgage on the precious property, but in the end wisely said no. West Virginia was a long way from our home in Upland, Indiana, and the Eden we imbibed would shortly cease to exist. Bulldozers and backhoes would soon insure that ours *was* in fact a "once in a lifetime experience." Fairways and palatial estates wouldn't be the same.

Have you ever had an experience of creation like that—when words seemed inadequate and silence alone seemed fitting? My guess is that you have, whether in the mountains or on the seashore, on a lake or in the woods, the morning after a fresh snow or late at night under the stars—or perhaps in awe of a stunning sunset.

I believe these sudden encounters with the sublime reveal an innate human awareness of God's revelation within nature, what the apostle Paul described as God's eternal power and divine nature—God's invisible attributes that we can still detect in creation today (Rom 1:20).

Biblical Eden

Years and years before our trip to West Virginia, my first mental contact with biblical Eden came from the lips of my mother as she read aloud Ken Taylor's *The Bible in Pictures for Little Eyes*. The long rectangular book reduced the Bible to short episodes, fascinating pictures, and simple questions. There was nothing I loved more than blurting out answers to these questions faster than my little brother, David. Competitive from the crib, I proved the truth of the fall at every developmental stage—despite my mother's persistent efforts.

The Bible stories made their impressions, however. With the first picture, I saw God moving above waters through a dark cloud-encircled tunnel that stretched toward the light of sun rays at the other end. God's mysterious power was comforting, yet scary at the same time. Falling in the black waters of creation in the dead of night was strangely terrifying.

The second and third pictures were idyllic depictions of the Garden of Eden. These were a little less impressive, perhaps because they didn't seem as real or maybe because they weren't scary.

I recently opened a library copy of Taylor's book to refresh my memory. Remarkably, the images instantly restored childhood impressions from forty years before. The beautiful world of Eden included an elephant, a peacock, two deer beneath a palm tree, a parrot, an alligator, a jumping fish, and purple flowers similar to ones I'd seen in our neighborhood. Of course, David and I had liked it that the animals weren't eating one another. They were friendly.

In the third picture Adam and Eve stood at a distance gazing up through beams of light toward heaven. They stood behind a bush of yellow flowers, so we couldn't see their naked bodies. A resting leopard looked on kindly from beneath the shade of a plant similar to the trees in my dinosaur books. There were two large deer, one with antlers like one of Santa's reindeer, and another jumping fish.

And such was Eden. It was ok but not exciting—not to little boys who lived on baseball and TV episodes of Daniel Boone. I would find far more interesting the next story about the Devil and the fall, then Cain and Abel, Noah and the ark, the Tower of Babel, Abraham's talk with God beneath the stars, Jacob's wrestling match with an angel, and on and on. The creation story, not seeming entirely real or entertaining, soon lost my interest.

Today I have the impression that many Christians view the creation account in similar terms. Genesis 1–2 is a text of poetic truth that stands at the periphery of Christianity's pillar doctrines. Saving faith in Jesus Christ is what really matters—not one's beliefs about creation. Evolution, Intelligent Design, Creationism, harmonization of Adam and the dinosaurs—"that stuff just doesn't really interest me" . . . "And I'm not really that interested in studying the biblical theology of creation—I remember it from childhood" . . . "the scientists and fundamentalists can battle it out—let's move on to the meaty issues of justification and the atonement!"

Such thinking, however, comes at the expense of biblical theology, where creation is literally the beginning and the end of all that the Bible reveals—including justification and the atonement (as we shall see later in chapter 4). For the theology of creation is essential for understanding the character of God, the incarnation of Jesus, miracles, biblical ethics, the resurrection from the dead, and the biblical hope for our physical world—the new heavens and the new earth.

Genesis 1:1 tells us that God by his very nature *is* creative. To dispense with God's unique creative power is to undermine God's invisible attributes, eternal power, and divine nature (Rom 1:20). As University of Chicago theologian Langdon Gilkey put it, "creation is that activity of God by means of which we define what we mean by the word 'God.'"[1] Indeed, for herein do we find the rationale for the believability of the entire Christian faith. If God created in the beginning, then it remains plausible that God can, if he wills, create again and again throughout history in the events we refer to as miracles.

1. Gilkey, *Heaven and Earth*, 83.

With this simple insight, the truth of Christianity falls into place. God's incarnation of supernatural life in the womb of the Virgin Mary was an extension of his power to create. God's resurrection of Jesus demonstrated that his power to recreate surpassed the destructive power of death. The Holy Spirit's spontaneous generation of the church on the day of Pentecost was an act of creation. And God's recreation of the heavens and the earth will vindicate once and for all God's cosmic creative power. He will overcome evil with good. It's all possible and plausible, if God really is the creator God. For the resurrection of the dead and the restoration of the natural world are essentially God's acts of recreation. His breathing of the Holy Spirit within believers is a faint echo of his original creation of Adam and Eve and, at the same time, a faint foreshadowing of the future resurrection. Creation pumps the lifeblood of faith and proclaims the vitality of Jesus' saving power:

> In the beginning was the Word, and the Word was with God, and the Word was God. He was in the beginning with God. *All things came into being by Him, and apart from him nothing came into being that has come into being.* (John 1:1–3)

> And he is the image of the invisible God, the first-born of all creation. *For by him all things were created, both in the heavens and on earth, visible and invisible.* (Col 1:15–16)

What prophets of neighboring faiths can compare? Jesus comes forth as God in the flesh, "Immanuel," God with us, with the creative power to turn water into wine, heal the crippled, cleanse sinners, and resuscitate the dead. Jesus is *unique*, the only one of his kind, because he has the power to recreate (John 1:14). Only upon an encounter with the Creative Word *who created in the beginning* can one be "born again."

Such is the logic of the Bible, where there is both a creation Christology and a creation soteriology—a sophisticated way of saying that Christ is God's agent of creation (creation Christology) and that salvation happens through God's creative power (creation soteriology; *soter* is Greek for "savior"). Biblically speaking, God's power to create is thus directly related to his power to save. What God created, he is able to fix.

It shouldn't be a surprise, therefore, that the very first sentence of the Apostles' Creed and the very first sentence of the Nicene Creed both frame Christianity upon the foundation of creation:

The Apostles' Creed

"I believe in God the Father Almighty, *Maker of heaven and earth.*"

The Nicene Creed

"I believe in one God the Father Almighty, *Maker of heaven and earth, and of things visible and invisible.*"

The Nicene and Apostles' Creeds identify God's creation of the heavens and the earth as the point of departure for ecumenical (church-wide) consensus. Originating at the font of church history, creation theology is thus an essential belief professed today by Orthodox, Catholic, and Protestant Christians alike.[2] Unity in the body of Christ begins with the doctrine of creation.

Faith in God as creator has always been the point of departure for Christian belief, because reality as we know it begins with the miracle of creation. It is for this reason that creation is the point of departure for Paul's evangelism among the gentiles in Lystra (Acts 14:15–17) and in Athens (Acts 17:24–29). It is also for this reason that the perversion of creation is the point of departure for Paul's doctrine of sin in Romans 1:18–32. And it is for this reason that creation is the inspiration for cosmic worship in Revelation 4:11: "Worthy are you, our Lord and our God, to receive glory and honor and power; for you created all things, and because of your will they existed and were created."

Physical creation *is* a reality. Spectacularly complex life *is* a reality— not the pastel pictures I looked at as a child, but the exhilarating reality of DNA as it spirals perfectly within the trillions of cells that form the human body. Beckley, West Virginia, was real and so too is the reality that we are wonderfully and beautifully made. Reality presupposes a miraculous beginning to our world.

Even the atheist, whose worldview depends upon a "cosmic accident" in which amino acids coincidentally smashed together to generate primitive life forms that evolved throughout millions of years, faces the reality that the spontaneous generation of even the simplest life is foreign to human experience, impossible to duplicate, and presently beyond the reach of scientific comprehension. We can't explain it. Life forms in our

2. Still broader, we may add that creation is one of the few doctrines that Christians have in common with both Jews and Muslims. Getting our direction from the Bible itself, creation is the natural place to begin evangelistic conversation with our fellow monotheists.

world simply do not simultaneously generate. As Paul Davies, "arguably the most influential contemporary expositor of modern science,"[3] attests: "the problem of how meaningful or semantic information can emerge spontaneously from a collection of mindless molecules subject to blind and purposeless forces presents a deep conceptual challenge."[4] Building on a quotation from philosopher David Conway, former atheist Antony Flew concurs:

> The first challenge is to produce a materialistic explanation for "the very first emergence of living matter from non-living matter. In being alive, living matter possesses a teleological organization that is wholly absent from everything that preceded it." The second challenge is to produce an equally materialistic explanation for "the emergence, from the very earliest life-forms which were incapable of reproducing themselves, of life-forms with a capacity for reproducing themselves. Without the existence of such a capacity, it would not have been possible for different species to emerge through random mutation and natural selection."[5]

Yet life in all of its complex, beautiful forms is an amazingly true *reality*. From where did life emerge if not from God?[6]

In this sense, the Bible is about reality, not the existence of what isn't real, but the restoration of what once was, the *re*creation and perfection of what presently is, and the revelation of what shall be. Yes, it is a faith, but it is a faith that reality requires. It is a seeing, thinking faith.

How is Genesis to be read? . . . literally? . . . figuratively? . . . as history? . . . as poetry . . . as myth? Yes, of course, careful analysis of literary form and authorial intent is essential to valid interpretation. But when the dust of scholarly debate settles and the latest academic fad fades, Genesis remains exceptional because Genesis is the point of departure for understanding Scripture. *Genesis is the foundation for biblical theology*.

With the rest of the Bible, Genesis is classified as Scripture—writing that is "inspired by God and profitable for teaching, for reproof, for correction, for training in righteousness; that the man or woman of God may be adequate, equipped for every good work" (2 Tim 3:16–17).

3. As quoted by Flew, *There is a God*, 111.

4. "The Origin of Life II: How did it Begin?" Quoted from Flew, *There is a God*, 129.

5. Flew, *There is a God*, 125–26, quoting Conway, *Rediscovery of Wisdom*, 125.

6. For a description of the major views on the origin of life, see Meyer, *Signature in the Cell*, 11–57 and Flew, *There is a God*, 113–21, 133–45.

This truth, too, is essentially undeniable in academic terms. Genesis has not been transmitted through the centuries because of its value for science or literature or history but entirely because of what it has been to generations of past believers—*sacred Scripture* that instructs believers in their relationship with their Creator. This being incontrovertible, 2 Timothy 3:15 presupposes Genesis as one of the "sacred writings which are able to give the wisdom that leads to salvation through faith which is in Christ Jesus."

Herein, for the Christian, lies the primary importance of Genesis—it is the point of departure for understanding God, wisdom, humanity's relationship to God, and the logical rationale for the believability of biblical truth—including salvation. For this reason the New Testament author of Hebrews explains, "By faith we understand that the worlds were prepared by the word of God, so that what is seen was not made out of things which are visible" (Heb 11:3). And Paul makes exemplary Abraham's belief in the God, "who gives life to the dead and calls into being that which does not exist" (Rom 4:17). Scripture itself thus entreats us to view faith and understanding of physical reality as interrelated. To dispense with one limits understanding of the other.

Personal experience of God, the joy of salvation, cosmic design in nature, the spectacular complexity of life, and the extra-physical abstract realities of love, joy, grief, conscience, and beauty are difficult at times to believe and yet they are all too real to be the coincidence of unguided inanimate materialism. Faith in these abstract realities is not a figment of the imagination or the effect of artificial stimulants. Too many intelligent human beings have attested their reality throughout history to pass them off as mere superstition. Faith is not "make believe."

To the contrary, as many have argued, good science supports the principle of creation. The word *science* derives from the Latin *scire*, which means "to know." The empirical fact that every known creation derives from a preexisting creator[7] in a cause and effect relationship makes the claim that God created the heavens and the earth plausible. No one doubts that even anonymous poems, paintings, inventions, or buildings were the creations of a creator's imagination and construction; they were not simultaneously generated as a consequence of random inanimate

---

7. Intelligent Design theory, whatever one's opinion, has an undeniably valid starting point with this simple premise.

materialistic coincidences. Indeed, one may infer that common sense suggests this truth as self-evident.

Of course there is a diversity of opinion among Christians about creation, but, as we have seen, all Christians agree that the atheistic model is less compelling *intellectually* than a model in which God created the universe and the life within it.

The generalization, for example, of Oxford zoologist and renowned atheist Richard Dawkins is simply not intellectually persuasive:

> In a universe of electrons and selfish genes, blind physical forces and genetic replication, some people are going to get hurt, other people are going to get lucky, and you won't find any rhyme or reason in it, nor any justice. The universe that we observe has precisely the properties we should expect if there is, at bottom, no design, no purpose, no evil, no good, nothing but pitiless indifference.[8]

No design? No purpose? No evil? No good? Is this thinking true to reality? Is it truly intuitive and rational? Dawkins's atheistic faith requires that we believe in sheer coincidence as the explanation for all reality, including life in all of its balanced complexity. What seems so real—the design of the human eye, the purpose behind parenting, the good of peace, and the evil of genocide—are all illusions according to Dawkins. Dawkins's atheistic model is strangely *unscientific* in this respect, because it calls for us to believe the irrational—not only that life just suddenly came forth from lifeless matter, but that deep life is itself a meaningless illusion. He requires that we disregard what we *know* to be true. Is that knowledge?

Could it be that folks like Dawkins suffer the real impairment? As a man's inability to see color does not disprove the existence of color but only that particular man's colorblindness, so might it be with the atheists' inability to see God.[9] Perhaps it is the *unimpaired* that see and the impaired that don't.

The end of the matter is that honest, objective Christians have the challenge of discerning what to believe in, while engaging respectfully with non-believers who hold to other schools of thought. For critical thinkers the optimal posture is one of open-minded interest in all schools

8. Dawkins, "God's Utility Function," 85.

9. Analogy taken from Richard Swinburne, "Justification of Theism," lines 331–32. For a reader friendly but thorough defense of the existence of God, see Craig and Moreland, *Philosophical Foundations*, 463–500. For a rigorous logical defense of the existence of God, see Swinburne's *Existence of God*.

of thought, with the guiding objective being the delineation of truth from falsehood. The choice is not between faith and science but for faith and science—rigorous science motivated by passionate faith.

What is unacceptable is uncritical dismissal of competing schools of thought that are suspect because they question popular consensus. Uncritical dismissal of Darwinian evolution,[10] Intelligent Design,[11] Creationism,[12] or any other theory of origins is unscientific and reproachable.

It is a rare thinker today—scientist, theologian, or lay person—who has comprehensively and objectively sifted through the respective arguments of Creationism, Intelligent Design, and Darwinian evolution. Far more common is dogmatic foreclosure based on subjective bias, external indoctrination, or inherited bias. If we are created in God's image, we can do better.

The biblically informed Christian will never pit faith against science, because the Christian call is to worship God with all of one's heart, but also with the entirety of one's mind (Mark 12:30). Rigorous exacting critical thought is as important to the informed Christian as deep devotional experience. Both are expressions of worship when we balance them

---

10. Representative theistic evolutionists include Oxford philosopher Richard Swinburne, prolific evangelical theologian and molecular biologist Alister McGrath, and renowned geneticist and head of the human genome project Francis Collins. Christian models of micro-evolution (theories that presuppose evolution within species) and even macro-evolution (theories that presuppose evolution from one species to another) identify God as the generating cause and sustainer of the evolutionary process: "Evolution could appear to us driven by chance, but from God's perspective the outcome would be entirely specified" (Collins, *Language of God*, 205). It is this rationale that inspired Arthur Peacocke, distinguished molecular biologist turned Anglican priest, to author *Evolution*.

11. Stephen Meyer's *Signature in the Cell* is an essential read for all engaged in this discussion. A brilliant scholar and engaging speaker, he holds a Ph.D. in the philosophy of science from the University of Cambridge.

12. Creationists cite an absence of intermediate fossil forms between evolutionary stages, the Second Law of Thermodynamics, and inaccurate radioactive dating of rocks and the universe as major flaws in the hypothesis of macro-evolution. "Since the second law states that entropy (disorder) will increase in any closed system over time, the increase in order and complexity during evolution seems to be in violation of this law" (Fowler and Kuebler, *Evolution Controversy*, 225). Moreover, creationists find it problematic that the New Testament identifies Adam as a literal human being rather than a figurative symbol, as the theory of Theistic Evolution requires (see Luke 3:38; Rom 5:12, 14; 1 Cor 15:22–45).

properly. The enlightened Christian is wise to engage in critical thinking with aggressive enthusiasm while employing the ideal of critical thought as defined, for example, by the American Philosophical Association: "The ideal critical thinker is habitually inquisitive, well-informed, trustful of reason, open-minded, flexible, fair-minded in evaluation, honest in facing personal biases, prudent in making judgments, willing to reconsider, clear about issues, orderly in complex matters, diligent in seeking relevant information, reasonable in the selection of criteria, focused in inquiry, and persistent in seeking results which are as precise as the subject and the circumstances of inquiry permit."[13] Dogmatism, the infamous "refuge of the lazy mind," is a sure sign of obstinate faithlessness—not the thinking faith promoted by Hebrews 11:3.

The God of the Bible seeks worshipers who will worship him in spirit *and in truth* (John 4:24). This being the case, God invites intellectual scrutiny, because truly critical thought will eventually lead to God, if God truly is the creator and source of all truth. Science is to be relished. If the God of the Bible does exist, good science will eventually complement his comprehensive truth. Certain of divine truth, secure Christians have always pursued science with intellectual enthusiasm and rigor, viewing science as nothing less than a gift from God himself. Indeed, this seems to have been the motivating conviction of Galileo, Copernicus, Newton, and the truly great believing scientists through the ages, whose sane faith led not to "intellectual suicide" but to invigorating discovery.

When it comes to the subject of God, however, science is limited to the general revelation of nature and can go no farther, because finite, mortal humanity is logically incapable of classifying an infinite, immortal, spiritual God. God by his very nature takes us beyond science into the world of the unknown. For God to meet the demands of science would be for him to be physical and material and constrained by time—and thus not really God. Hence, to presuppose that science could measure God is to presuppose that God by definition could not exist—and that's dogmatism, not critical thought as the American Philosophical Society defines it above.

Along these lines we may question the logic of Pulitzer Prize winning astronomer and atheist Carl Sagan (1934–96), who admonished that

13. Facione, *Critical Thinking*, 2. This quotation is part of an American Philosophical Association statement on critical thinking wordsmithed by forty-six experts from the disciplines of philosophy and education.

the scientific method "may be all that stands between us and the enveloping darkness."[14] How, we may ask, is science equipped to deter the very real darknesses of racial conflict, genocide, slavery, and countless other expressions of human cruelty and relational breakdown? These *realities* cannot be reduced to the physical and material. If they could, they would be predictable and preventable. And while the origins of these vices cannot be tested and verified, they are every bit as real as a smoking test tube.

Genesis

In the midst of this discerning process, Genesis reveals truth that is essential for understanding the remainder of the Bible. Its claim is that God inspired an ancient Hebrew writer (or writers) to convey the simple truth that God created the universe with human life as its crowning glory. The extreme simplicity of the story is to be understood with respect to its audience. The nimble advantage of Genesis over a technical treatise is the fact that the basic message of Genesis is readily understood by young children today just as it was by the ancient primitive mind.

Scientific explanation of creation would have been incomprehensible to the ancients, as it would be to us today—lest we assume a posture of naïve arrogance. For just as an eighteenth-century scientist would be overwhelmed by twenty-first century nuclear physics, the Internet, and modern medical technology, so, too, would we be overwhelmed if we were directly exposed to advances that will be taken for granted two thousand years from now. Wouldn't it be presumptuous to think otherwise?

Two hundred years ago the greatest scientific intellects of the world would have staked their lives on the universal accuracy of Newtonian physics. Why not, since there were no known exceptions? But now, with the help of Albert Einstein, the bewildering reality is that Newtonian physics falls short of explaining reality that exceeds the speed of light. In 1958 it was axiomatic that light could not bend. But in 1966 laser optics bent light in every direction. In 1958 astronomers limited Saturn's rings to eight. But by 1974 that number increased to four hundred fifty. In 1958 scientists limited reproduction to mating. But by 1977 reproduction by cloning proved possible for frogs, mice, and sheep. We obviously have not

14. Sagan, *Demon Haunted World*, 434.

exhausted the unknown. What other corrective discoveries lurk in the future of science?

The simplicity of Genesis thus contributes to its effectiveness as Scripture. Communicating in a way that all people of every generation can understand, it imparts the crucial truth of God's original creation of our world and the life within it. Is this revelation less believable than the naturalistic conjecture that all of reality is the result of chance, the random collision of inert matter or the conjecture of endless multiverses whose number would make the "cosmic accident" conceivable?[15]

Why Things Were the Way they Were

Today, if we close our eyes and imagine what this world was like before humanly caused pollution, extinctions, and environmental disasters, we can perceive that this world was once breathtaking from one corner of the globe to the other—from continent to continent and from the surface to the depths of the sea. The planet earth was pure, healthy, and vigorous with life. And it was real, not fantasy.

In daylight, moist, rich, deep green vegetation of every variety would overwhelm the human senses. Sight, taste, smell, touch—all species were indigenous, natural, fascinating, and wondrously beautiful. There were no invasive species or foreign diseases brought in on cargo pallets. Infinite color lived and moved and breathed and sang. The skies and trees were filled with multitudinous colors of flock upon flock of singing birds. Trees chorused with the chatter of swinging, jumping mammals. Life exploded with invigoration. Seas, rivers, and streams swarmed with abundant, vigorous, fascinating life. Undisturbed oceans concealed power, color, and constant motion—all in perfect balance above an ocean floor of unimaginable beauty and color. The waters were pure and clean.

Even global cataclysms had positive effects. Cataclysmic events were not by definition natural evils, because neither human beings nor advanced animal life was there to experience trauma as their consequence.

---

15. Representative of contemporary scientific faith in chance is the following quotation of the French biochemist Jacques Monod: "Chance *alone* is at the source of every innovation, of all creation in the biosphere. Pure chance, absolutely free but blind, at the very root of the stupendous edifice of evolution: this central concept of modern biology is no longer one among other possible or even conceivable hypotheses. It is today the *sole* conceivable hypothesis" (*Chance and Necessity*, 112–13).

Today we don't consider a hurricane to be a natural *disaster* unless it destroys property and takes life. Out of harm's reach, a hurricane is an awesome and fascinating display of natural beauty—as are tornados, tsunamis, and volcanoes. Prior to humankind and the fall, cataclysmic occurrences in nature may in fact have had fortunate results in that they contributed to the production of the natural environment that became necessary for sustained human life. Regardless of one's theory of origins and prehistory, it is indisputable that creation was once exponentially cleaner and more diverse than it is now. It is equally indisputable that human beings have been primarily responsible for the contamination of nature.

But what about nature caused suffering among animals prior to the fall? Does the phenomenon not question the goodness of God? Notre Dame philosopher Alvin Plantinga has argued that prior to the fall it is *possible* that Satan was the agent responsible for natural evil.[16] From a biblical theological standpoint, Plantinga's argument has the support of Rev 12:7-9, where Satan—"the god of this world" (2 Cor 4:4) who "deceives the entire inhabited world" (Rev 12:9)—is thrown down to the earth along with his demons. Preceding Genesis 3, the event makes credulous evil activity on the part of Satan prior to the fall. Would not such activity be true to his destructive character and his antagonism toward God and his creation?

In truth, the question takes us into the realm of conjecture, because we are unable to calculate the level of suffering experienced by other life forms, especially those that are now extinct or greatly advanced by the passage of time. In the end, appeals to pre-fall manifestations of natural evil are incapable of discrediting biblical theology and the goodness of God. Even if we discard the culpability of Satan as untenable, it remains uncertain that prehistoric animals, plants, and microorganisms were advanced enough intellectually to truly experience a degree of suffering that might classify as evil. Evil both requires an intellectual, volitional agent and an intellectually traumatized victim. A brontosaurus with a brain the size of a walnut does not fit the latter category. Neither does a fish or an amoeba. And sympathies with contemporary animals are anachronistic—particularly domestic animals that have evolved from modern inbreeding. I'm of the opinion that cats, dogs, horses, and such do suffer

16. Plantinga, *God, Freedom, and Evil*, 57-58. See Webb, *Dome of Eden* for a book-length biblical and theological defense of this view.

now, but I'm not so sure that they had counterparts then of the same intellectual capacity. Evolution would seem to require that they didn't.

Evil, in the fullest sense, requires an evil being, who, devoid of any motive that might be defined as good, finds pleasure in traumatizing an unwilling victim. Did natural disasters traumatize emotionally capable creatures prior to the fall? Can we confidently say yes? Is the evidence persuasive?

The testimony of Genesis is that the natural world was once good because God created it that way. God, Genesis tells us, is above all else the creator of invigorating life, astounding beauty, spectacular design, cosmic space, and extraordinary detail. The true God of reality is a God of purity, richness, and perfection. His art lives and breathes and speaks. God is an awesome God, and all creation tells the story of his glorious reality. By contrast, the emergence of humanity has resulted in unprecedented evil both against natural and human life. Nothing in prehistory remotely compares to the premeditated intentional evils that humans have committed throughout history.

As Scripture, Genesis opens eyes to what once was, so that the wise might better anticipate what eventually shall be: "Things which eye has not seen and ear has not heard, and which have not entered the heart of man, all that God has prepared for those who love Him" (1 Cor 2:9).

Genesis thus overwhelmingly affirms the goodness of God's creation:

> Gen 1:4: "And God saw that the light *was good.*"
>
> Gen 1:10: "And God called the dry land earth, and the gathering of the waters He called seas; and God saw that it *was good.*"
>
> Gen 1:12: "And the earth brought forth vegetation, plants yielding seed after their kind, and trees bearing fruit, with seed in them, after their kind; and God saw that it *was good.*"
>
> Gen 1:18: "And God placed them in the expanse of the heavens to give light on the earth, and to govern the day and the night, and to separate the light from the darkness; and God saw that it *was good.*"
>
> Gen 1:21: "And God created the great sea monsters, and every living creature that moves, with which the waters swarmed after their kind, and every winged bird after its kind; and God saw that it *was good.*"

Gen 1:25: "And God made the beasts of the earth after their kind, and the cattle after their kind, and everything that creeps on the ground after its kind; and God saw that it *was good*."

Gen 1:31: "And God saw all that He had made, and behold, it *was very good*."

As Scripture, Genesis reveals the true nature of God's purity and righteous goodness. And so it was with this conviction that the apostle Paul explained: "For since the creation of the world his invisible attributes, his eternal power and divine nature, have been clearly seen, being understood through what has been made" (Rom 1:20).

According to the Bible, reality today is but a scarred contortion of what reality once was. But the truth remains that we live in a real world that evidences both the consequences of human pollution and the still apparent grandeur of creation's resilient power and beauty, where God's divine nature may still be clearly seen through what has been made.

Ironically, the reality of the world's inherent goodness—the problem of good—is an intellectual problem for those who reject Christianity because of the problem of evil. If a good God doesn't exist, where did good come from? From where does *agape* love come? From where did the concept of beauty originate? If reality is based on the phenomenon of the survival of the fittest, from where did the concept of self-sacrifice derive? If evil makes fantasy of God, how are we to explain the undeniable effectiveness of forgiveness and reconciliation? Forgiveness works. Why?

God's Benevolent Sovereignty in Creation

As Scripture that reveals wisdom leading to understanding, Genesis reveals that prior to human and Satanic disobedience, God exercised his power *benevolently* to prepare a perfect world for humanity to live in. Taking the reader behind visible creation to the creation event itself, Genesis teaches that God's creativity is a direct extension of his unique *sovereign* power. For in the absence of every other living being, God created a spectacular world for the dwelling of his eventual people.

Creation is God's premeditated, foreordained gift. Natural resources were not man's doing, they were simply there, God having already made them for humankind to enjoy as the sustaining pleasures of life. For the thinker steeped in Scripture, God's creativity is therefore inseparable from his premeditated love—creation being a gift of God's grace. Perhaps it's the godless worldview that requires "intellectual suicide." "Evil's greatest triumph may be its success in portraying religion as an enemy of pleasure when, in fact, all the things we enjoy are the inventions of a Creator."[17]

Herein is the origin of the abstract biblical concept of the kingdom of God. The kingdom of God is the sphere of God's active benevolent rule on behalf of his people. Defined in this manner, salvation was, in fact, the natural state of being for Adam and Eve before they sinned. They lived in perfect peace and harmony with God, with one another, and with nature in a perfect universe governed exclusively by God. Jesus' mission would be to restore this lost harmony and perfect rule to the people of God, salvation coming on the heels of the kingdom's arrival.

Through miracles of healing, cleansing, the feeding of the masses, and the resuscitation of the dead, Jesus' ministry would declare the presence of the kingdom of God. Like living, acted parables, Jesus' supernatural acts would herald the eventual restoration of God's original plan of creation. Motivated by love, God's power to save is thus an extension of his original power to create.

But that is the subject of a later chapter. For now we must not lose sight of the simple message. Genesis teaches that creation occurred because God commanded it through his *spoken* word. Creation was an act of communication between God and his future people who would be created in his image. Creation *was spoken* as a revelation to communicate what could not be known otherwise. Inherently, that message is that God is supreme in power as the exclusive agent of creation and that God is inherently good as creator of an originally perfect world. Nature thus continues to speak in the whispers (and sometimes thunders) that theologians refer to as general revelation.

Because benevolent sovereignty is the character of God, the reader of Genesis is at a loss to detect any evidence whatsoever of evil in God's action in Genesis 1–2. Designs for cruelty simply do not exist. It would be upon this premise of God's benevolent holy sovereignty that Judeo-Christian faith and worship would progress: "For you are not a God who takes pleasure in wickedness; no evil dwells with you" (Ps 5:4). "God is light, and in him there is no darkness at all" (1 John 1:5); "in him there is no sin" (1 John 3:5).

17. Yancey, *Orthodoxy*, xv.

Genesis thus reinforces the creative, revealing, benevolent power of God's word with each successive command:

"Then God *said*, 'Let there be light': and there *was* light.'" (Gen 1:3)

"Then God *said*, 'Let there be an expanse in the midst of the waters.'" (Gen 1:6)

"Then God *said*, 'Let the waters below the heavens be gathered into one place.'" (Gen 1:9)

"Then God *said*, 'Let the earth sprout vegetation.'" (Gen 1:11)

"Then God *said*, 'Let there be lights in the expanse of the heavens.'" (Gen 1:14)

"Then God *said*, 'Let the waters team with swarms of living creatures.'" (Gen 1:20).

"Then God *said*, 'Let the earth bring forth living creatures after their kind.'" (Gen 1:24)

"Then God *said*, 'Let us make man in our image, according to our likeness.'" (Gen 1:26)

As Scripture that reveals wisdom that leads to salvation, Genesis is thus a corrective to the intellectually challenged worldview of atheism. For, according to Scripture, to live by a godless worldview is to pursue illusion.

The perspective is *contemporary* and relevant. Is it really logical to think that inanimate inert matter randomly combined to initiate the process that engineered thinking, feeling, analytical human minds in bodies constituted of living cells replete with spectacularly sophisticated DNA? Is the prospect intellectually astute?

The biblical perspective is arguably more realistic, because it's intellectually easier to believe that intelligence created life than it is to believe that life just fell into place by undirected coincidence. Likewise, it's easier to believe that the human consciousness of good and evil is an innate result of our common heritage as creations of God, than it is to believe that everything that happens is the result of materialistic cause and effect—including all of our thoughts and actions whether good or bad.

It is here that Genesis provides the entry point for the gospel. By contrast to atheistic cause and effect materialism, Genesis maintains that humankind, though fractured, has a very real hope in its original creator, who alone has the power to heal and *re*create. Taking its cue from the foundational truth of Genesis 1–2, Psalm 100 thus calls believers to celebrate and worship the true God as benevolent, sovereign creator: "Know that the Lord himself is God; It is he who has made us, and not we ourselves. . . . For the Lord is good; His loving-kindness is everlasting, and his faithfulness to all generations" (Ps 100:3, 5). The Christian hope is that God will again exercise his love in the future—this time in re-creative power. What God created, he can fix.

The Value and Significance of Human Life

With an inherent value infinitely greater than mere "living tissue," Genesis places humankind at the center of God's perfectly balanced universe. Humanity is not the being of supreme worth and power, God is exclusively and immeasurably so; however, humanity has a unique place of prominence and responsibility in God's hierarchical order. For the arrangement of creation tells the story of God's unique love for humanity. Saving the best and most important for last, God created humanity alone in his image.

This simple revelation, largely unheeded by human history, affirms *both* genders as created in God's image. Neither male chauvinism nor radical feminism has its precedent in God's original design, where male and female complement and complete one another in a mutually beneficial relationship that is comprehensively good. The entire creation account climaxes in God's creation of man and woman in his image.

It is not the physical universe but humanity that receives special attention. Remarkably, the universe receives only the slightest passing notice—*he made the stars also* (Gen 1:16). The importance and value of humankind ascends to a devotion that surpasses both nature and physical matter (Psalm 8).

Equally evident is the reality of evil. Pharaoh's infanticides, Alexander's reign of terror, Herod's dysfunction, Hitler's holocaust, Stalin's gulags, Mao's mass-murders, Pol Pot's killing fields, Bin Laden's terror attack—they all instantly register as repugnant travesties of justice against humanity. These travesties repulse the human spirit as manifestations of sheer evil. Why?

The Bible's answer is that travesties against humankind are travesties against the true God who created human beings in his image. If created by God, human beings have a supernatural value, a meaningful conscience, an innate sense of morality, and a divine purpose. Because God created humanity and loves us all (from the least to the greatest), all "crimes against humanity" are crimes against the Creator of humanity. Ethics thus derive from creation. The human conscience communicates humanity's creation in the image of God.

Were we but stardust—as popular atheists glibly surmise—a holocaust would be of little significance. In the cosmic scheme of things, what would be the loss of a few million units of animate carbon? If the moral conscience is not real, who can say that the pragmatic Darwinian "survival of the fittest" strategies of Hitler, Stalin, and Mao were wrong? Were they not playing their natural roles within the Darwinian progress of our species by eliminating undesirable DNA?

In the Likeness of God

What does it mean that God created man and woman in his own likeness? To some degree this question is a mystery. Clearly humanity is not all-knowing, all-powerful, and infinite in space and time as God is. Such attributes are not features of humankind—either as portrayed in the Bible or as we experience life today.

God created humanity with the potential for decision making, for contemplation, for emotion, for communication, for responsibility, for engaging in imaginative, creative invention. Like God, human beings have a mind, a soul, a spirit, emotions, and a will. Christians concur with the Westminster Shorter Catechism that the chief end of humankind "is to glorify God, and to enjoy him forever." Humanity has the potential for deeply intimate relationships with one another and with God. In each of these aspects, humanity is distinct from the rest of creation. And it is in these respects that humanity has its chief purpose, so that Jesus identified the greatest commands as the love of God and the love of neighbor (Matt 22:37–40).

Created in God's image, human beings, like God, have a free will. It is a freedom, however, that God apportions to human beings within the dimensions of space and time. Human beings are thus subject to the laws God has created within nature. We cannot, for instance, transcend gravity or resist the passage of time. We are subject to the law of death. Our free will is also subordinate to the justice and final judgment of God—we are responsible to God for how we exercise our freedom, whether in sin or obedient faith. Hence, human freedom is neither a challenge to nor a compromise of God's eternal sovereignty or God's uniqueness as God. Just as human partial knowledge does not lessen God's omniscience, and as limited human power does not detract from God's omnipotence, neither does limited human freedom detract from God's absolute freedom and eternal sovereignty. God has displayed his sovereignty in creating human beings who have the freedom to make responsible decisions.

Simple Revelation

Genesis is written from a simple perspective in non-technical terms as a father would describe the world's origins to his children. The words are true and comprehensive without being beyond the reach of their intended audience. There is no attempt to be scientific or technical, exacting or precise in minute detail. Such is not always the purpose of Scripture. Revealing the wisdom that leads to salvation, Genesis speaks to the human mind and soul of God's unique placement of humanity at the center of creation. The simplest truths are the most important and profound. It was in part for this reason that Jesus told his disciples, "unless you turn and become like children, you shall not enter the kingdom of heaven" (Matt 18:3).

Genesis speaks to the childlike curiosities of the human soul: light, darkness, night, day, the waters, the heavens, the dry land, the plants, the seeds, the sun, the moon, fruits and vegetables, the birds, the fish, sea creatures, animals, and, ultimately and climactically, the human race itself. God created all this with vitality and astonishing beauty for humanity to live in and with. In reality such beauty does evoke wonder and awe. For in the reality that we live, conscious human beings do experience God's grandeur "in the dearest freshness deep down things."[18] And in the discovery of God's grandeur we discover humanity's precious value—not mere tissue, but God's chief creation inherent with a living loving soul. We have a conscience.

Yet many throughout history have found God's infinitude and universal presence intimidating and difficult to harmonize with any kind of interest that God might have for humanity. How could a God so expansive and powerful love a human race that is so incredibly small by

18. Gerard Manley Hopkins, *God's Grandeur*, line 10.

comparison? From a purely scientific perspective, we are, as Carl Sagan put it, very small: "We live on a hunk of rock and metal that circles a humdrum star that is one of 400 billion other stars that make up the Milky Way Galaxy, which is one of billions of other galaxies which make up a universe which may be one of a very large number, perhaps an infinite number, of other universes."[19] "We float like a mote of dust in the morning sky."[20]

Sagan was right of course. What do people look like from the top floor of the Empire State Building, or from the window of a jet at thirty thousand feet, or from a satellite in space? We grow smaller and smaller before vanishing altogether against the ever expanding space of the universe. We are very, very small. Does such not suggest our ultimate insignificance?

The Bible tells otherwise. David, Israel's most famous king, was aware of this sobering reality: "When I consider your heavens, the work of your fingers, the moon and the stars, which you have ordained; what is man, that you take thought of him?" (Ps 8:3–4). Yet, David's contemplation didn't lead to despair. Contemplation of the created universe led him to the revelation first discovered in Genesis—namely, that God has subordinated all creation to humankind:

> What is man that you take thought of him? And the son of man, that you care for him? Yet you have made him a little lower than God [NIV: angels], and have crowned him with glory and majesty! You make him to rule over the works of your hands; you have placed all things under his feet, all sheep and oxen, and also the beasts of the field, the birds of the heavens, and the fish of the sea, whatever passes through the paths of the sea. (Ps 8:4–8)

Nature's subordination to humanity didn't lead David to hope in humanity's ability to sustain itself—an ancient form of secular humanism. David's meditation led to the worship of God, who had *given* humanity its special place of prominence: "O Lord, our Lord, how majestic is your name in all the earth!" (Ps 8:1, 9). And David's elevation of humankind didn't come at the expense of God's glory but in affirmation of human beings *as creations in the image of the true God of ultimate glory.* Thus we see both in biblical revelation (Rev 4:11) and in the human experience of nature (my West

19. Quoted from ABC *Nightline with Ted Koppel*, December 4, 1996.
20. Sagan, *Cosmos*, 4.

Virginia experience), that creation itself inspires worship. True worship is not an isolated subjective emotion but an inspired response to the reality of God's revelation: "Worthy are you, our Lord and our God, to receive glory and honor and power; for you created all things, and because of your will they existed, and were created" (Rev 4:11).

The Call to Creation: Human Responsibility

In the beginning God gave Adam and Eve a calling infused with meaning and purpose: "And God blessed them; and God said to them, 'Be fruitful and multiply, and fill the earth, and subdue it; and rule over the fish of the sea and over the birds of the sky, and over every living thing that moves on the earth'" (Gen 1:28). Adam and Eve didn't invent meaning and artificially project it onto the world to create purposeful existence like twentieth-century existentialists.

Meaning and purpose was inherent within them. With God's blessing, they were stable emotionally and psychologically. Like well adjusted children, Adam and Eve had not just the approval but the full blessing of their God and Father. They had the inner joy of knowing God's pleasure in them and the liberating knowledge that God was glad they existed—for like all creation, they were *very good* (Gen 1:31).

Moreover, they had the security of knowing what their calling and purpose was. They didn't have to contrive purposeful existence. They discovered meaning in their relationship with God, with one another, and in everything they did. Remarkably, their calling was to do what they most wanted and desired—to populate the earth and tend God's awesome creation. They had responsibility in the best of all imaginable senses: to do what they were designed and created to do. Herein Scripture reveals the inherent goodness of exhilarating monogamous sexual intercourse and fulfilling, satisfying work. At its inception, Scripture reminds us, human life was satisfying, fulfilling, exhilarating, and exceedingly abundant. Populating and stewarding the earth was a gift, a calling, and a desirable responsibility.

For Christians this worldview is more *intellectually satisfying* and *true to life* than the atheistic faith that there is no inherent purpose and meaning in life, no good and no evil, except for what people artificially invent. Having thought deeply on this question, the Christian conviction is that the deep realities of the human soul are not an illusion.

Conclusion

Genesis teaches that creation is the beginning of the "gospel," the *good* news that God is good, creation is inherently good, and humankind, though now diseased with sin, bears God's image and is also good by original design.

Is there hope for this fractured, polluted world of endless conflict? If God is the creator of our world, if he still has the power to *re*create, and if he still values and loves his creation, there remains hope that he will act again to forgive, heal, and recreate in order to accomplish his original purpose. This revelation about God is the first feature of wisdom that leads to salvation. That this is in fact the plan of God is the message of the gospel of Jesus Christ: "For God so loved the world, that he gave his only begotten son, that whosoever believes in him should not perish, but have eternal life" (John 3:16); "I came that they might have life, and might have it abundantly" (John 10:10).

Yes, that all sounds wonderful, the skeptic retorts—but why, then, are things so terribly bad? If God is so good, and if God is so powerful, why does his chief creation suffer such misery? It is to this important question that we now turn in chapter 2.

Questions for Discussion, Further Study, and Meditation

- Why does the Bible begin with the story of creation?

- How does the creation story of Genesis 1–2 prepare the reader of the Bible to understand the concept of the kingdom of God?

- How does creation theology prepare the reader of the Bible to understand the doctrine of salvation?

- What are the major obstacles to believing in God's creation of life?

- Identify and describe your experiences in nature that suggest the reality of God's existence. If you have not had such experiences, how do you explain the experiences of others who have? If you have had them, how do you explain the absence of such experiences by others?

- Is it conceivable in your mind that life as we know it could be the result of unthinking random physical coincidences? Why or why not? What arguments oppose the conclusion you have reached and why aren't they persuasive?

- Renowned atheist Richard Dawkins has made the statement that our world is exactly what you would expect it to be if there were no God. Do you agree with that statement? Why or why not?

- If you accept Intelligent Design theory, how would you respond to the questions of atheist Robert G. Ingersoll? "Who can appreciate the mercy of so making the world that all animals devour animals; so that every mouth is a slaughterhouse, and every stomach a tomb? Is it possible to discover infinite intelligence and love in universal and eternal carnage?"[21]

- To a limited degree, this chapter integrates biblical theology with apologetics (the defense of an established position—in this case the Christian faith). In your opinion, is that integration a weakness of this chapter, or is apologetics a necessary component already inherent within biblical theology? Might it be said that Genesis was, from the beginning, a defense of Yahweh's creation of the heavens and the earth in contradistinction to competing pagan worldviews?

21. Ingersoll, "Gods," 1.70–71.

Suggested Scripture Reading

Genesis 1–3, 9; Job 38–42; Psalms 8, 19, 148; Proverbs 8; Isaiah 40:9–31; 65:17–25; Luke 8:22–25; John 1:1–18; 5:19–30; 15:1–11; Acts 17:16–34; Romans 4:17; 8:18–30; Colossians 1:15–20; 2:1–23; Hebrews 1:1–14; 2 Peter 3:3–16; Revelation 21:1–8.

2

It's a Humpty Dumpty World:
Sin and its Consequences

Humpty Dumpty sat on a wall

Humpty Dumpty had a great fall

All the King's Horses

And all the King's Men

Couldn't put Humpty together again!

The famous nursery rhyme, Humpty Dumpty, probably originated from the Battle of Bosworth, which took place in 1485 between England's King Richard III and Henry Tudor, the head of the house of Lancaster. At the battle of Bosworth Field, Richard III, made famous by Shakespeare's play, fell from his horse named "Wall" and was subsequently hacked to pieces. Though a simple nursery rhyme, Humpty Dumpty tells a profound truth. All egocentrics like Richard III eventually self-destruct on the path of self-aggrandizement.

With a few qualifications, Humpty Dumpty symbolizes the human race in the real world as we know it. Ever present in contemporary reality are the irreversible consequences of humanity's shattering fall. Watch the evening news. Story after story discloses the tragedy of senseless injustice. Ours is a fractured world.

The Serpent

The universe is still unspoiled when Genesis 3 begins. Paradise is intact and all relationships are intimate and peaceful. Into this idyllic scene comes the most "crafty" beast that the Lord God had made. Satan sneaks on the scene to turn Adam and Eve against God. Tragically, he succeeds and the result is the convulsion of creation, shameful separation from God, and the fracturing of all relationships.

And all the world's gold, all the world's temples, all the world's idols, all the world's drugs, and all the world's counselors would never be able to put Humpty together again. There would be no quick fix. There would be no substitute for the true creator God. Weak and false imitations would come and go, but there would be no other God.

As Scripture that gives wisdom that leads to salvation, Genesis 3 reveals the nature of sin and evil. The initial revelation is simply that Satan exists. He is at large and his purpose is cruel, insidious, and destructive. The serpent is *anti-God*. His objective is not to test, to refine, and to discipline for humanity's ultimate good. He's not God's right-hand man. His purpose, rather, is to destroy. His premeditated plan is to harm. Keenly aware of this reality, Jesus would portray Satan for who he really is: "a murderer from the beginning" (John 8:44). Genesis thus reveals the truth that there is real destructive evil in the world of reality. It's not an illusion. And its consequences are catastrophic.

Satan, however, is not sovereign. Genesis 3:1 informs us that the serpent was one of the creatures of the field *that God had made*. Satan himself is thus evidence of how far a creature can plummet from their original design as a creature of God. Revelation 12 recounts that Satan (the dragon) was cast out of heaven by the angel Michael for leading an insurrection against God. Satan thus prototypically epitomizes sin and the disease of character that can deform a creature of God into a sin-hungry beast.

But as a created being, the serpent is greatly limited in power by comparison to the Creator. Because he can't take God on directly, he has to act covertly through crafty seduction and cunning lies. Even when his sinister plan works, he, like Adam and Eve, is powerless against God's punishment.

The serpent, therefore, is not God's evil equal. Michael's triumph in Revelation 12:9 reduces Satan to a defeated inferior whose likeness to

God is limited to his supernatural identity. In all other respects, he is a weak, false, evil imitation:

> And there was war in heaven, Michael and his angels waging war with the dragon. And the dragon and his angels waged war, and they were not strong enough, and there was no longer a place found for them in heaven. And the great dragon was thrown down, the serpent of old who is called the devil and Satan, who deceives the whole world; he was thrown down to earth, and his angels were thrown down with him." (Rev 12:7–9)

Elsewhere in the Bible, Satan's vincibility is further evident when the epistle of 1 John congratulates young men who themselves have triumphed over Satan: "I have written to you, young men, because you are strong, and the word of God abides in you, and you have overcome the evil one" (1 John 2:14).

With these complementary biblical revelations before us, it is important to observe that the serpent *does not overpower* Eve and Adam in Genesis 3 through frontal assault. He seduces and deceives them through *deceptive words*. By contrast to God's word—which created beauty, purity, companionship, and abundant life—Satan's words deceive, defame, and divide. His words purport to supersede God's creative truth, but they are in fact destructive lies.

What could the serpent have said that could have compelled Adam and Eve to risk paradise and intimacy with God? With stealth, Satan spoke words of persuasion in the form of insidious inquisition: "*Indeed, has God said, 'you shall not eat from any tree in the garden?'*" (Gen 3:1). Satan, as his name means, is a slanderer. Steeped in slander, his simple but carefully crafted question begs a disobedient *yes* answer.

And the human preference for "yes" is part of Satan's deception. Yes is usually a positive, affirmative answer that people like to say—much more so than an uncomfortable confrontational "no."

But the yes Satan seeks is *not* a good yes. Just the opposite—Satan desires to coerce a disobedient and even defiant yes—"Yes, God is unfair; yes, God's prohibition about the tree is unreasonable; yes, God is legalistic; yes, it *would* be to our advantage to disobey God; yes, God cannot be trusted."

Initially, however, Eve evades Satan's ploy. Still innocent, she responds with tentative correction: "From the trees of the garden *we may eat*; but from the fruit of the tree which is in the middle of the garden, God has said 'You shall not eat from it or touch it, lest you die'" (Gen 3:2–3; compare 2:16–17). *Well done Eve—way to go!*

Subtly, however, Satan has succeeded in planting the first seed of human doubt in God's goodness. Eve considers for the first time that God might not be looking out for her best interests.

Hastily keeping the conversation going, Satan then fires a blatant lie: "You surely shall not die!" (Gen 2:4). Knowing full well that Adam and Eve *would* indeed die, the serpent emerges Satanic. For he knew that God's word was always the whole truth and nothing but. His deception exposes his cruel evil nature, as Jesus' assessment further attests: "He was a murderer from the beginning, and does not stand in the truth, because there is no truth in him. Whenever he speaks a lie, he speaks from his own nature; for he is a liar, and the father of lies" (John 8:44). Satan's *anti-God* lie was a malicious misrepresentation of reality. The wages of sin would indeed be death as God forewarned, and as Satan had experienced, so too would Adam and Eve suffer separation from God as a consequence of their sin.

Though he is not, Satan speaks *as though* he is God's equal by claiming the very mind of God: "For God knows that in the day you eat from it your eyes will be opened, and you will be like God, knowing good and evil" (Gen 3:5). This statement is a partial truth and therefore a complete lie. Allowing Revelation 12 to inform our reading of Genesis 3, Satan knew the consequences of disobeying God because he had had the experience of disobeying God himself—"your eyes will be opened" and "you will know good and evil." That much was true. But in the fullest sense, it was categorically untrue that Adam and Eve would be like God as a consequence of eating the forbidden fruit. Just the opposite—they were already created in the image of God—sin would result in their becoming less and less like God. Their disobedience would result in defiling ruin and the contamination of their God image. The reward for their sin would be fractured relationship and psychological and emotional shame. Unlike every other creature God had made, Adam and Eve would have to cover their nakedness.

As Scripture that leads to wisdom, Genesis thus reveals the power of the spoken word—both for supernatural good and supernatural evil (compare Jas 3:6–12). Genesis attests that there is such a thing as malicious falsehood that is intended to divert from truth and cause destruction. In the real world, not all roads lead to truth, prosperity, and enduring pleasure. The wise understand that words must be critically evaluated before they are trusted and acted upon. To claim the mind of God is not only absurd pretension but also a diabolical evil that ties directly to *false* prophecy. *Adam and Eve would indeed die.*

Adam and Eve

Adam and Eve did grow in wisdom and understanding with respect to good and evil, but it was not a desirable growth. It was not a wisdom that led to spiritual and relational prosperity and enduring health. One might compare their discovery to the disillusionment that a soldier discovers in the savage realities of war. Yes, the soldier discovers, there is savage evil and horrible, unjustified, unspeakable suffering in this world of reality. Soldiers do turn up missing in action to never reunite with their families. Combat trauma does carry over to drug addiction and sometimes to suicide. Combat missions do go wrong resulting in collateral damage and significant loss of civilian life. Yes the soldier does grow in knowledge with respect to these realities. But that is not desirable knowledge that leads to abundant life. It is altogether different from "the wisdom that leads to salvation through faith which is in Christ Jesus" (2 Tim 3:15).

Or one might compare Adam and Eve's discovery to that of the countless who seek to satisfy their sexual appetites through pornography. As with the forbidden fruit, the sight of pornography arouses hunger for something that is morally destructive and contrary to the design of God. Pornography ignites fanciful sexual intercourse with an image, an explicit form of adultery according to Jesus (Matt 5:27–28). Pornography not only perverts God's creative design for sexual union within marriage (Gen 2:24), but it also reduces the individual photographed to the status of an impersonal stimulant. What God designed as the wonderful consummation of the most intimate of human relationships, pornography perverts into a shameful addiction. The result is separation from God, psychological and emotional shame, and frustration in never discovering physical satisfaction in sexual intercourse as God designed it for marriage. Such is the nature of evil. Pornography is a weak, false imitation of physical sexual intercourse between committed loving partners in the covenant of marriage. To violate God's design is to miss out on the fullness of his blessing.

Thus, analogous to the fall of Adam and Eve, war and pornography both provide stimulation, and yet neither produces an edifying discovery that leads to an abundant life. Both are destructive. And when twisted in the carnal passions of satanic perpetrators, each results in collateral damage that extends to millions of innocent people—as the pointless slaughters of Alexander the Great, Napoleon, Hitler, and Stalin proved, and as the international sex trade demonstrates today (most pointedly in the evils of sex slavery and child pornography). In each case the discovery of the knowledge of good and evil is nauseating and disturbing.

In these respects, Adam and Eve's lament in *Paradise Lost* is most relevant:

> . . . since our Eyes
> Op'n'd we find indeed, and find we know
> Both Good and Evil, Good lost, and Evil got,
> Bad Fruit of Knowledge, if this be to know,
> Which leaves us naked thus, of Honour void,
> Of Innocence, of Faith, of Puritie,
> Our wonted Ornaments now soiled and stained,
> And in our Faces evident the signes
> Of foul concupiscence; whence evil store;
> Ev'n Shame, the last of evils.[1]

Such was the empty "wisdom" gained—a wisdom that did not lead to salvation but to misery.

Hardly innocent dupes, Adam and Eve were fully responsible sinners. Their acts of disobedience displayed their inner faith*lessness*, their prioritization of selfish interests, and the limitation of their devotion to the God who created and truly loved them. The Devil did *not* make them do it! They had the power to stand firm as we may infer from 1 Corinthians 10:13.

Of course, Adam and Eve believed in God and in his existence, but they did not believe in God with relational faithfulness, obedience, and love, which alone matter when it comes to security in the kingdom of God. As we shall see in the next two chapters, saving faith is a relationship between committed, faithful partners. In the end, Adam and Eve were fully responsible for their sin—they were not faithful, obedient, or trusting— and hence God was fully just in his punishment of them.

1. Shawcross, *Complete Poetry of John Milton*, 1070–79.

But what was the great crime in partaking of a forbidden fruit? Didn't God unreasonably tempt them by putting the seduction right before their eyes?

Such surface level questions miss the gravity of the crime. Like Satan, Adam and Eve desired to be *like* God. As the apostle Paul would later explain, they, *unlike* Jesus, considered "equality with God something to be grasped" (Phil 2:6). And so they rejected God's word, engaged in the fantasy of Satan's lies, put themselves above God, and obeyed their appetites for power and illicit pleasure. In so doing, they themselves became *anti-God* and became like the serpent. Hence, they suffered expulsion from Eden as Satan had experienced expulsion from heaven. They became sinners in a now hostile world of chaos. Paradise was lost.

"Does Something Catch Your Eye?"

Bazaars in the Middle East are renowned for their deep, narrow shops with floors and walls attractively covered with items "to attract the eye." Tourists without the slightest intent on buying a thing are often "taken in" by the attraction of handsomely crafted souvenirs of silver, bronze, ceramic, mother of pearl, ebony, olive wood, and silk. Like impulse buys the world over, these purchases are often later regretted as unaffordable extravagances.

On a far grander scale, such was the mistake of Adam and Eve: "When the woman saw that the tree was good for food, and that it was *a delight to the eyes*, and that the tree was desirable to make one wise, she took from its fruit and ate; and she gave also to her husband with her, and he ate" (Gen 3:6).

Adam and Eve did not eat from the forbidden tree because their stomach juices were churning with hunger. Their cup overflowed with endless bounty—the entire garden was theirs for food. And they did not eat because the other trees in the garden were unattractive, for all the trees were "pleasing to the sight and good for food" (Gen 2:9). Rather, this fruit was attractive to their eyes expressly because it was forbidden. The desire of their eyes was a *covetous* desire for what they didn't need, what they did not yet have, and what God had temporarily forbidden.[2] In feeding

2. It is interesting to note that the Bible does envision God's eventual permission to eat of the tree of life: "To him who overcomes, I will grant to eat of the tree of life, which is in the paradise of God" (Rev 2:7).

this covetous hunger, they rejected God's will knowingly and exchanged God for the desires of their flesh (Gen 2:17). *The desire for what they did not have became their god.* And so they exchanged the true living God for an imagined, non-existent falsehood—that reality apart from God could be better than reality with God. History has evidenced the tragedy of this exchange. The fallen world of Genesis 3 would devolve into the dysfunction of Romans 1:18–32.

As Scripture that gives wisdom that leads to salvation, Genesis reveals the alternative to life with God. Revealing the consequences of sin, Scripture goads the reader from destruction to pursue the restoration of God's original design for abundant life and intimate relational trust. By contrast to Satan, Jesus would come to restore the abundant life of the kingdom of God: "The thief comes only to steal, and kill, and destroy; I came that they might have life, and might have it abundantly" (John 10:10).

The Original Cover Up

Adam and Eve exchanged intimacy with God for the shame of selfish ambition:

> Then the eyes of both of them were opened, and they knew that they were naked; and they sewed fig leaves together and made themselves loin coverings. And they heard the sound of the Lord God walking in the garden in the cool of the day, and the man and his wife hid themselves from the presence of the Lord God among the trees of the garden. Then the Lord God called to the man, and said to him, "Where are you?" And he said, "I heard the sound of you in the garden, and I was afraid because I was naked; so I hid myself." And He said, "Who told you that you were naked? Have you eaten from the tree of which I commanded you not to eat?" And the man said, "The woman whom you gave to be with me, she gave me from the tree, and I ate it." Then the Lord God said to the woman, "What is this you have done?" And the woman said, "the serpent deceived me, and I ate." (Gen 3:7–13)

Adam and Eve instantly knew they were naked, vulnerable, and insecure. The phenomenon of *cover up* entered human history. No longer inherently good, Adam and Eve needed clothes to mask their shame.

Infected with guilt, Adam and Eve "hid themselves from the presence of the Lord" (Gen 3:8), and for the first time their eyes were opened to the phenomenon of fear—"I was afraid because I was naked; so I hid" (Gen 3:10). The one who had been their loving life source was now their enemy and judge. Once holy, perfect, and innocent, they were now prisoners of their own sin and guilt. Their state of depravity was such that they sought the darkness among the trees rather than the light of God's exposing presence. In so doing they epitomized the human race: "Everyone who does evil hates the light, and will not come into the light for fear that his deeds will be exposed" (John 3:20).

God's Reaction to Adam and Eve's Sin

How does the God who created the heavens and the earth respond to disobedience? In language clothed with anthropomorphism, Genesis presents God "walking in the garden" to visit and *counsel* his children. Like the serpent before, God initiates conversation with a question, "*Where are you?*" (Gen 3:9).

But God's question, unlike Satan's, does not aim to seduce or deceive but to prompt confession. God comes as wonderful counselor. His question probes deeper than physical location. Of course God knows *exactly* where Adam and Eve are. This is a question of the heart. You were with me before. *Where are you now?* "Adam and Eve, *where* are you?"

God's second question probes still more deeply: "*Who told you that you were naked? Have you eaten from the tree of which I commanded you not to eat?*" (Gen 3:11). In this confrontation between truth and falsehood, Genesis reveals that "the word of God is living and active and sharper than any two-edged sword, and piercing as far as the division of soul and spirit, of both joints and marrow, and able to judge the thoughts and intentions of the heart. And there is no creature hidden from his sight, but all things are open and laid bare to the eyes of him with whom we have to do" (Heb 4:12–13). Adam's heart is laid bare before God. And God knows exactly where Adam is. There is no pretense, beating about the bush, or playing mental games. God knows exactly what Adam has done and graciously gives Adam the opportunity to come out with it.

In this swift and subtle interplay, the reader of Genesis discovers another universal reality—the reality of the human conscience. Innately, Adam sensed his nakedness and felt shame. The serpent had not told him that he was naked, Eve had not told him, and God had not. Adam himself was guilty and he felt it innately. So it is that to have a conscience is to be truly human. Honesty, truth, and justice are not inventions of the human imagination but universal realities known innately by creatures who bear God's image.[3]

Yet, overwhelmed by God's penetrating two-part question, Adam dodges self-exposing confession, the only commendable action he could have taken, to place blame back on God and on his close companion, lover, and dearest friend, Eve—"The woman whom *you* gave to be with me, *she* gave me from the tree, and I ate" (Gen 3:12).

In betraying God and now Eve, Adam isolates himself from divine and human relationship to break what would later be revealed as the two commandments upon which the whole law and the prophets would be built: "You shall love the Lord your God with all your heart, and with all your soul, and with all your mind. This is the great and foremost commandment. The second is like it, you shall love your neighbor as yourself. On these two commandments depend the whole law and the prophets" (Matt 22:37–40).

Unfaithful to the first command, Adam is swift to compromise the second. To save face, he excuses his sin at Eve's expense: "the woman whom you gave to be with me, she gave to me from the tree and I ate" (Gen 3:12). In a freefall from purity to self-destruction, Adam crashes into the uncompromising holy character of God. To protect his pride, he spurns the love of God and the love of neighbor. And all is lost. Humpty is shattered.

With Adam sobered to the reality of his sin, God now asks just one question of Eve—"What is this *you* have done?" (Gen 3:13). Graciously, God does not phrase the question as a multiple choice set of options. Clearly and directly he identifies Eve as a member of the anti-God conspiracy: "What is this *you* have done?" As he had done with Adam, God gives Eve the opportunity to confess her sin. And to her credit she essentially does, though she too saves partial face by blaming the serpent— "The *serpent* deceived me, and I ate" (Gen 3:13).

As Scripture that gives wisdom that leads to salvation, Genesis 3 depicts God immediately reacting to sin with patient grace and unmerited

---

3. It's interesting to note that the universal phenomenon of the conscience played a major role in the altered worldviews of both C. S. Lewis (*Mere Christianity*) and Francis Collins (*Language of God*).

love. Remarkably, the Creator of the universe values his relationship with humanity to the extent that he acts to confront Adam and Eve to engage in potentially reconciling dialogue. *God asks questions!* And with all benevolence he gives his unfaithful children the opportunity to confess their mistakes and come back to him. He patiently delays his wrath to provide further opportunity for repentance.

This revelation about God is another feature of wisdom that leads to salvation: "If we say that we have no sin, we are deceiving ourselves, and the truth is not in us. If we confess our sins, he is faithful and righteous to forgive us our sins and to cleanse us from all unrighteousness. If we say that we have not sinned, we make him a liar, and his word is not in us" (1 John 1:8–10).

Who are the wise in this world, but those who confess their sins before acting to reconcile their broken relationships? It is in this direction that Scripture aims to lead us. God's word speaks instructions that lead to confession, repentance, reconciliation, and rebirth.

Divine Punishment

But grace will not come cheaply. As sacred Scripture that gives wisdom that leads to salvation, Genesis discloses that God's love is wedded to his pure truth, so that it is God's very nature to maintain truth by revealing falsehood and exposing the destructive consequences of sin. God is judge by his very nature and demonstrates his sovereignty by punishing the sins of responsible persons. God's righteous justice affirms truth, defends the innocent, and preempts further destruction. On the other hand, God's toleration of injustice would compromise his own holy character and render impossible the restoration of humanity to its perfect design in his image (Lev 19:2). Punitive judgment is thus an essential feature of God's plan of redemption.

Refining discipline was the only alternative to capital punishment, if God was to act in love without compromising justice. And so, in punishing Adam and Eve, God acted as a father lovingly and graciously disciplining his children for the sake of humankind's *eternal* well-being. As George MacDonald put it, "He is against sin: insofar as, and while, they and sin are one, he is against them—against their desires, their aims, their fears, and their hopes; and thus he is altogether and always *for them*."[4]

4. Lewis, *George MacDonald*, 4.

Intolerant of deception, God acted with disciplinary love to expose falsehood and initiate reconciliation: "For whom the Lord loves he reproves, even as a father, the son in whom he delights" (Prov 3:12).

Thus God conclusively refuted Adam's insinuation that the chain of responsibility for sin went back to God himself—"the woman whom *you* gave to be with me, she gave me from the tree." God justly placed the blame entirely on the shoulders of the three parties involved:

> "*Have you eaten* from the tree of which *I commanded you not* to eat?" (Gen 3:11).

> "What is this *you have done*?" (Gen 3:13).

> "Because *you have done* this" (Gen 3:14).

> "*Because you have listened* to the voice of your wife" (Gen 3:17).

Satan, Eve, and Adam were the exclusive primary agents of the original sin. God's punishment of the three parties is therefore entirely just, which it would *not* have been if God had in some way stimulated or caused their acts of disobedience. Such logic undergirds the Christian worldviews of Augustine and Anselm:

> **Augustine:** Certainly, for evil could not have come into being without a cause. However, if you ask what the cause may be, I cannot say, since there is no one cause; rather, each evil man is the cause of his own evildoing. If you doubt this, then listen to what we said above: evil deeds are punished by the justice of God. It would not be just to punish evil deeds if they were not done willfully (*De libero arbitrio voluntatis*).[5]

> **Anselm:** Because the apostate angel [Satan] and the first man [Adam] sinned by their own choice which was so free that it could not be compelled by any other thing to sin, each of them sinned by free choice. Therefore, each of them is justly blamed because in spite of having this freedom of choice, each sinned freely and out of no necessity and without being compelled by anything else. However, each sinned by his own choice, which was free; but neither sinned by means of that in virtue of which his choice was free (*De Libertate Arbitrii* ch. 2).

> You do not doubt that the Devil sinned, since he was not able to be unjustly damned by a just God (*De Casu Diaboli*, ch. 4).

---

5. Augustine, *On Free Choice of the Will*, 3.

Necessitating such conclusions, Genesis reveals that God originally designed human beings in his own image with the capacity to make "first cause" decisions for which they would be held responsible. Thus God's sovereignty is such that he is able to create willful beings who can make first-cause decisions of their own. Apart from this reality, God's judgment and his commendation would make no sense. However, in accord with biblical truth, human obedience toward God results in blessing, while disobedience results in punitive judgment (Deut 30:15–20; Matt 25:31–46). The Bible presupposes this simple reality right up to its conclusion in the book of Revelation: "And I saw the dead, the great and the small, standing before the throne, and books were opened; and another book was opened, which is the book of life; and the dead were judged from the things which were written in the books, according to their deeds" (Rev 20:12). God reveals his sovereignty not through causing everything that happens, whether good or bad, for such would make God's judgment irrational and unjust. According to Scripture, God reveals his sovereignty in creation, in the truth and power of his inspired word, in his eternal supremacy over the transient powers of history, in his final judgment of all responsible persons, and ultimately in the resurrection of the dead and the recreation of the heavens and the earth. Thus God in his sovereignty will overcome evil with the greater power of divine love.

Why Things Are the Way They Are

Genesis reveals that evil is a consequences of sin, and the punishing consequences of that sin survive to this day (Gen 3:14–19). Reality as we experience it is impacted by the Humpty Dumpty crash of the fall. Human relationships *are* challenging. And the natural world *is* chaotic and unpredictable. Natural catastrophes *do* happen. The earth *does* produce thorns. It does take tremendous effort to farm. Even with the greatest efforts of science and technology, drought, floods, and plagues still render humanity helpless. Women do suffer childbirth. And, lest we be naïve, unprovoked evil flourishes in our world today. We live in a world of conflict between nations, between races, between genders, between husband and wife, and even within our own disturbed minds. Dysfunctional conflict is a daily reality.

The Universal Consequences of Adam's Sin

The reality of sin is an axiom of orthodox Christianity. Jesus and Paul speak of human beings as "slaves" to sin (John 8:34; Rom 6:17, 20). Paul speaks of "the law of sin" (Rom 7:23, 25; 8:2) that emerged from Adam: "as through one man sin entered into the world, and death through sin, and so death spread to all men, because all sinned" (Rom 5:12). Later Augustine avowed, "all have sinned in that first man, because all were in him at that time when he sinned, and that from then on sin is inherited through birth" (Augustine [354–430], *Contra duas Epistolas Pelagianorum*, 4.4, 7).[6]

According to Romans 1:18–32, things are the way they are for this reason. The real world is tragic. Uncensored history is an R rated story unfit for pleasant conversation. And honest Christians who are informed by Scripture and uncensored history are sober to the fact. The Turkish massacres of Armenians in WWI, the holocaust of the Jews in WWII, Stalin's gulags, Mao's mass murders, Pol Pot's killing fields, the Rwandan and Sudanese massacres, 9/11, the Lord's Resistance Army, the contemporary sex trade—none of these travesties are surprising to the biblically and historically literate. Why? Because the *reality* is that history, perhaps especially biblical history, reveals a wisdom that anticipates human violence and dysfunction: this is a "perverse generation" (Acts 2:40); the present age is "an evil age" (Gal 1:4); "all is vanity under the sun" (Eccl 1:14).

In this respect, as elsewhere, Scripture is true to reality. Of Adam and Eve's children, one is the first to murder and the other is the first to be murdered.[7] Then history follows Cain's example: "From there, the history of sin and corruption moves on, down the ages, in a cast of billions."[8] All violence is domestic violence. We're all related. Crimes against humanity

---

6. It is important to note, however, that Augustine went beyond Pauline theology to conclude that original sin has passed from one generation to the next through physical procreation, so that each human being is culpable for the sin of Adam and therefore worthy of eternal punishment—even when that human being is an infant who dies before accountability. At this point, we may legitimately question Augustine's faithfulness to Paul, as Romans 5:12 seems to place blame on responsible sinners: "just as through one man sin entered into the world, and death through sin, and so death spread to all men, because all sinned."

7. As observed by Marshall, *Heaven is Not my Home*, 29.

8. Plantinga, *Engaging God's World*, 53.

are crimes against us. Those who think otherwise are rightly thought of as beasts—they are not fully human.

And so it is that biblical history is violent from the start. In the Exodus, the Israelites experience enslavement, infanticide, and forced exile—hardly utopia. God's covenant people then suffer severe oppression at the hands of the Assyrians and the Babylonians. Then, behind the scenes of Second Temple Judaism, Alexander the Great's legacy is one of ruthless terror and unbridled fornication—history fit for adult viewers only.

Thereafter the experience of God's New Testament people proves no different. Jesus is born during Herod's reign of terror (Matt 2:16–18); John the Baptist is beheaded; *Jesus is crucified*; Stephen is stoned; James is beheaded; Peter is jailed; Paul suffers a tortuous life of discomfort and unjust persecution prior to his final arrest (2 Cor 11:23–28); the author of Revelation suffers exile on Patmos, while the followers of Jesus face severe persecution at the hands of the Roman emperor cult. Only through radical faith does Christianity emerge from the corrupt, brutal age of Roman rule.

Christian Hypocrisy and the Truth

The Bible makes plain that *God's people are prone to sin like everyone else.* In this respect modern defrockings of celebrity Christians fits into a long sullied scandalous tradition. The Bible itself reports of the ancient Hebrews performing child sacrifice (Jer 7:31), engaging in male and female cult prostitution (1 Kgs 14; 2 Kgs 17 and 23), and constantly falling prey to the seduction of idol worship (Isa 2). Perhaps the low point comes in Ezekiel's comparison of the people of Judah to a whore who spreads her legs to every passer-by (Ezek 16:25). Yes, it's right there in the Bible.

On the individual stage, it was Moses' brother Aaron, the first high priest, who fashioned the infamous golden calf (Exod 32:1–4). And the kings of Israel and Judah were notoriously corrupt—David's scandal with Bathsheba being just one moral failure among many.

Hence, scandalous behavior among God's people is not fresh news. Like the Israelites before them, the earliest Christians suffered fractious sins from within. Paul's first letter to the Corinthians is a virtual catalog of that church's moral shortcomings—divisive conflicts, fornication, drunkenness, gluttony, bitter lawsuits, religious arrogance, abuse of sacred rites, and outright denial of the resurrection of Christ—hardly faith generating expressions of salt and light.

For the biblically informed, it is therefore not at all surprising that Christian leaders are sometimes caught in sin, that Christians have to work at marriage like everyone else, that Christians succumb to pornography, that Christians can be racist, and sometimes just plain stupid. For such realities are fully anticipated by the Bible itself. Ironically, as G. K. Chesterton put it: "one of the strongest arguments in favor of Christianity is the failure of Christians, who thereby prove what the Bible teaches about the Fall and original sin. As the world goes wrong, it proves that the church is right in this basic doctrine."[9]

Indeed, short of full obedience to God through the enabling of the Holy Spirit, all are potential perpetrators of evil: "*all* have sinned and fall short of the glory of God" (Rom 3:23). Such is the reality of the contemporary church. The truth is, as Randy Alcorn puts it, "A Christ-centered church is not a showcase for saints but a hospital of sinners."[10]

What About Natural Disasters

The Bible is equally *realistic* at the prospect of natural catastrophes. The harm caused by tsunamis, hurricanes, tornados, earthquakes, droughts, and indiscriminating plagues are expected repercussions of the fall. Paradise is lost. Creation itself groans for redemption (Rom 8:22). As Scripture that leads to wisdom, the Bible depicts this world as a hostile place (Gal 1:4), often characterized by chaos rather than harmony within nature. Plagues and famines are thus a recurrent feature in the Bible itself. Cosmos is a hope for the future, not an expectation for the present (Isa 11:6–9; Rom 8:19–22).

Therefore neither human atrocities nor natural disasters come as a surprise to the Christian informed by Scripture. Each is to be comprehended as a tragic consequence of original sin. Humanity has had destructive tendencies ever since Adam. Because rebellion against God originally had cosmic physical consequences, the natural world still suffers chaos—"*cursed is the ground because of you*" (Gen 3:17). We yearn for something better,

9. As quoted by Yancey, *Orthodoxy*, xix.

10. Alcorn, *Heaven*, 35.

> For the anxious longing of the creation waits eagerly for the reveal-
> ing of the sons of God. For the creation was subjected to futility,
> not of its own will, but because of him who subjected it, in hope
> that the creation itself also will be set free from its slavery to cor-
> ruption into the freedom of the glory of the children of God. For
> we know that the whole creation groans and suffers the pains of
> childbirth together until now. (Rom 8:19–22)

Inhumane Sins

Granting the continued consequences of the fall, how are we to explain
spectacular sins—real life inhuman acts of perverted bestiality like child
prostitution and hardcore pornography? How can these things happen, if
all human beings are created in the image of God?

The phenomenon is haunting. But it is not surprising to one informed by the Bible. Leviticus 18 catalogs XXX-rated vices that would
cause a pimp to blush—"you shall not have intercourse with any animal
to be defiled with it, nor shall any woman stand before an animal to mate
with it; it is a perversion. Do not defile yourselves by any of these things;
for by all these the nations which I am casting out before you have become defiled" (Lev 18:23–24). In the New Testament Paul's worldview is
equally sober and realistic:

> And in the same way also the men abandoned the natural func-
> tion of the woman and burned in their desire toward one another,
> men with men committing indecent acts and receiving in their
> own persons the due penalty of their error. And just as they did
> not see fit to acknowledge God any longer, God gave them over
> to a depraved mind, to do those things which are not proper, be-
> ing filled with all unrighteousness, wickedness, greed, evil; full of
> envy, murder, strife, deceit, malice. (Rom 1:27–29)

The Bible is thus fully aware of moral evil and is not uninformed with
regard to its contagious threat. "A little leaven leavens the whole lump"
(1 Cor 5:6).

The Dehumanization of the Self

In 1940 Walt Disney produced the classic animated film *Pinocchio*. Based
on the original book by Carlo Collodi, the puppet Pinocchio famously

transforms into a real boy by proving himself "brave, truthful, and unselfish." The film, like the book, is saturated with moral insights, many of which correspond with Scripture. In Jiminy Cricket, Pinocchio discovers a conscience, "a still small voice" that gives him wise direction against the foolish temptations he faces from one adventure to the next.

Pinocchio lives in a world of moral absolutes where his lies become as obvious as the nose that grows on his face. He discovers life only after he has given his own to save his father Gipetto, who had been swallowed by the great whale Monstro. Finally, after being pronounced dead, Pinocchio comes back to life not as a puppet but as a real boy—born again into a superior reality. Fittingly, the story concludes with Gipetto putting on a great celebration for the rebirth of the one he had originally created. Tragedy becomes comedy; death gives way to transformed resurrected life. And the end of the story is a party.

The connection for us, however, occurs in the middle of the film when Pinocchio strays to Pleasure Island—a place of reckless abandonment and juvenile unrestraint. He befriends Lampwick, a hell-bent scoundrel, who pressures Pinocchio into smoking, drinking, gambling, and all kinds of juvenile behavior. Then, to Jiminy Cricket's horror, the boys suddenly begin to take on visible features of jackasses. First their ears, then their tales, then their voices, until finally Lampwick metamorphoses into a literal beast, a jackass that is sold into work at a local salt mine.

The moral of the episode is that bestiality is a gradual process that begins with defiant feeding of sensual appetites. Pinocchio's adventure finds biblical precedent in Daniel's description of the Babylonian king Nebuchadnezzar, who deformed into a beast as punishment for his defiance of God:

> But when his heart was lifted up and his spirit became so proud that he behaved arrogantly, he was deposed from his royal throne, and his glory was taken away from him. He was also driven away from mankind, and his heart was made like that of beasts, and his dwelling place was with the wild donkeys. He was given grass to eat like cattle, and his body was drenched with the dew of heaven, until he recognized that the Most High God is ruler over the realm of mankind, and that He sets over it whomever he wishes. (Dan 5:20–21)

Nebuchadnezzar's self-absorbed appetite for power rendered worship of the true God impossible, so that he became a senseless, insane beast.

The apocalyptic message is a symbolic statement of a supernatural law of human degeneration—all who defy God to worship their appetites (for power or anything else) will gradually devolve into a state of bestiality. They will always lose their senses—it's a law of reality.

In the New Testament a similar phenomenon characterizes the beast of Revelation 13: "Here is wisdom. Let him who has understanding calculate the number of the beast, for the number is that of a man; and his number is six hundred and sixty-six" (Rev 13:18). The number *is the number of a man*, probably Nero, whom the earliest Christians remembered as a vicious, cruel persecutor of God's people.[11] Nero—like Pharaoh, like Nebuchadnezzar, like Napoleon, like Hitler, like Stalin, like Osama Bin Laden—was a beast. Intoxication with power together with a deranged worldview dehumanized each of these villains with the result that they each perpetrated beastly acts of destructive terror.

Bestiality, therefore, does not come as a surprise to the biblically informed. To the contrary, it is a documented dysfunction that has characterized extreme forms of self-worship throughout history.

Sin against Creation is Sin against God

How do our first two chapters interrelate? To answer this question, we turn to Psalm 51 where King David seeks God's forgiveness for his scandalous affair with Bathsheba, his botched cover up, and his traitorous murder of Bathsheba's husband, Uriah.

In the fourth verse of this famous Psalm, David unexpectedly professes: "Against you, you only, I have sinned, and done what is evil in your sight."

"Hold on," the contemporary reader responds, "how can that be true?" "Didn't David sin egregiously against Uriah?" "Didn't he sin against Uriah's family?" "Didn't he betray Uriah's comrades and the trust of the whole Israelite army—indeed the entire nation?" "And, admittedly, while it takes two to tango, didn't he bear the burden of the responsibility for seducing Bathsheba in the first place?" So how can it be said that David sinned against God only?

11. Richard Bauckham has substantiated at great length the centuries-old association of 666 with Caesar Nero. He concludes: "The gematria does not merely assert that Nero is the beast: it demonstrates that he is. Nero's very name identifies him by its numerical value as the apocalyptic beast of Daniel's prophecy" (*Climax of Prophecy*, 389).

Reasoning along these lines is understandable and is indeed true to contemporary theological conviction, as evidenced most pointedly by the holocaust survivor and profound author, Ellie Wiesel, who outspokenly maintains that there are some sins God cannot forgive, like the holocaust, because some sins are not against God but against human beings.[12] If forgiveness is to take place, it's the victim of sin who suffers the burden of forgiveness, not God. In David's case, that would mean the family and friends of Uriah. In the case of the holocaust, that would mean the contemporary Jewish people.

As reasonable as this may sound, this line of thinking displays the fallacious consequences of making a theological judgment independent of the control of comprehensive biblical theology grounded in God's identity as sovereign creator. I humbly submit that what Wiesel doesn't consider is God's intimate relationship to the victims of the holocaust— that every individual murdered was a creation of God that God loved intimately. And if biblical revelation is true, God loved each holocaust victim more than did their own closest relatives and more than Wiesel himself. God was their creator and had the most to lose in their destruction. More than that, Hitler's sins were in direct defiance of God's revealed law that prohibits murder. Hitler's actions were anti-God and their consequences were categorically opposite God's sovereign plan for reconciliation of Jew and Gentile (Eph 2:11–18; Gal 3:28). In the holocaust, God was violated most and thus has the most to forgive.

The same is true of David's sin. David violated God's design for monogamous marriage (Gen 2:24; Matt 19:5). David violated God's desire for "truth in the innermost being" (Ps 51:6). David violated God's prohibitions of murder and adultery. David violated the trust of *God's* people. And in murdering Uriah, David destroyed a human being—God's chief creation.

And so it is with all violence. Violence against creation is violation of God. I submit that this revelation comes as a rebuke to contemporary American evangelicals, who rightly condemn illicit sexual content in popular entertainment but at the same time regularly find entertainment in graphic violence. *Is commandment six less important than commandment seven?*

---

12. Wiesel, *Power of Forgiveness*.

Conclusion

The phenomenon of evil does not necessitate intellectual rejection either of God's existence or of God's character as an all-powerful and all-loving God. The Bible reveals that God is not indifferent to the suffering of our world. He suffers too. As doctor Paul Tournier insightfully put it, "The suffering of man is also the suffering of God. That is always my reply to those who tell me that they can't believe in God in the face of all the suffering that goes on in the world. God is the greatest sufferer; the state of the world causes him so much suffering that we are told that 'it repented the Lord that he had made man on the earth, and it grieved him at his heart' (Genesis 6:6)."[13]

Indeed, what is the message of redemption, but God's action through Christ to eliminate evil so as to bring peace and comfort to those in pain— that tears might be wiped away (Rev 21:4)? As we shall see in chapter 4, according to plan, God will defeat evil with sacrificial love.

Considering all the ink that has been spilled over Christianity's supposed inability to deal with the problem of evil, it is indeed an irony that the problems of sin and evil prove far more difficult for atheistic worldviews than they do for the biblically informed. For while the Bible defines sin and evil as rebellious acts of disobedience against God and fellow human beings (the conscience bearing evidence of our creation in God's image), atheistic models fail to explain the human conscience, guilt, and the debilitating trauma of relational breakdown. Are these abstract realities to be attributed to purely physical and materialistic cause and effect—predetermined reflexes of our morally disinterested DNA? Or is the biblical explanation more persuasive—that the realities of pain, suffering, evil, and death attest to the truth that something is wrong in our world that needs to be set right? The gradual unfolding of God's strategy for solving this problem takes the form of an innate reality shared by all human beings—the need for trusting, enduring, committed relationships—the heart's desire for family and relational intimacy. It is to this subject that we now turn.

13. Tournier, *Reflections*, 171–72.

Questions for Discussion, Further Study, and Meditation

- Is sin a reality? If you answered yes, define sin in your own words. If you answered no, explain your understanding of the concept's origin: where does the concept of injustice come from?

- Atheists often appeal to evil as a basis for disproving either the goodness or the omnipotence of God, thinking that God would intervene to prevent evil if he were both all-loving and all-powerful. What is your response to this age old enigma?

- Biblical revelation suggests that all human beings are created in God's image yet still inherit a sinful nature at birth. How do you explain the origin and continued coexistence of this tension?

- How is it possible for unbelievers to do good things and for believers to do bad things?

- According to the biblical accounts, what compelled Satan and then Adam and Eve to sin? In what ways is the same temptation still a danger for contemporary people?

- If God created Satan, Adam, and Eve, was he not responsible for the crimes they committed? Why or why not?

- Contemporary history is replete with sensational evils in the forms of genocide, religious terrorism, slavery, and the global sex trade. How does biblical revelation provide a foundation for understanding these tragedies?

- What is your response to John Stuart Mill's criticism that Christianity is legalistic and negative? "Christian morality (so called) has all the character of a reaction; it is, in great part, a protest against paganism. Its ideal is negative rather than positive; passive rather than active; innocence rather than nobleness; abstinence from evil rather than energetic pursuit of good; in its precepts (as has been well said) 'thou shalt not' predominates unduly over 'thou shalt.' In its horror of sensuality, it made an idol of asceticism which has been gradually compromised away into one of legality."[14]

14. *On Liberty*, 112.

Suggested Scripture Reading

Genesis 3, 6–8, 11:1–9; Numbers 14; Deuteronomy 28–32; Exodus 32;
Leviticus 16, 18; Judges 1–3, 20; Psalm 51; Nehemiah 9; Isaiah 1–6, 24,
28–29; Jeremiah 2–7, 48; Ezekiel 11, 16, 20; Romans 1–3, 6; 1 John 3, 5;
Revelation 2–3, 9, 18.

3

The Covenant Solution: It's All About Relationships

God's Covenant with Noah

Few Bible stories are more familiar to the secular reader than the story of Noah. The ark, the bearded old man, animals arrayed two by two, and the bold colored rainbow find modern markets ranging from toys and children's books to fabric designs and wallpaper. The ancient story is a cozy part of our contemporary culture.

But what does it mean in its biblical context? A closer examination reveals that the Noah episode is anything but a warm and cozy fairy tale. Indeed, it is the most countercultural account of God's wrath in the whole Bible. What contemporary natural disaster could compare? For here, apart from Noah and his family, we are dealing with the drowning of the entire earth's population. Such is the seriousness of sin and the foreboding reality of God's wrath.

Yet the Noah story is at the same time a story of God's grace and his action through an agreement with Noah to advance God's plan both for creation and for humankind. Still further, the story is the beginning point for understanding God's successive covenants with Abraham, Moses, David, and the prophets of the "new covenant"—most notably Isaiah, Jeremiah, Ezekiel, and Hosea. Each covenant builds on its predecessor in moving history toward the perfection of God's original plan to live intimately with his people in a world uncontaminated by the effects of sin.

The story of Noah looks back towards creation and forward into the vast history to follow. With respect to the former, the flood of Genesis 6–9 is a reversal of creation. As David J. A. Clines has observed, "The flood is only the final stage in a process of cosmic disintegration that began in Eden."[1] Whereas God had originally separated the waters from the dry land (Gen 1:9), in the Noah account "the great deep burst open, and the floodgates of the heavens were opened" (Gen 7:11). Whereas God had originally taken pleasure in Adam and Eve (Gen 1:27–31), in the Noah account he grieves over his creation and voices regret for having made humanity: "then the Lord saw that the wickedness of man was great on the earth, and that every intent of the thoughts of his heart was only evil continually. And the Lord was sorry that he had made man in the earth, and he was grieved in his heart" (Gen 6:5–6). Whereas Genesis 1–2 reveals the wonder of God's creation, the Noah story depicts the destructive global consequences of sin: "And the Lord said, 'I will blot out man whom I have created from the face of the land, from man to animal to created things and to birds of the sky; for I am sorry that I have made them'" (Gen 6:7). Whereas God had formerly brought order out of nothingness, he now rains forty days of chaos and death—a global affirmation of the reality of God's wrath and the destructive nature of sin.

But there is a silver lining. God acts unilaterally to maintain his original plan by preserving Noah's family along with the animals on the ark. God, by his grace, preserves his creation through a relationship with one man: "But I will establish my covenant with you; and you shall enter the ark—you and your sons and your wife, and your son's wives with you" (Gen 6:18). This commitment of God to Noah is, by definition, a covenant—"a solemn commitment guaranteeing promises or obligations undertaken by one or both covenanting parties."[2] God promises Noah and all of creation that he will not again destroy the inhabitants of the earth by flood, offering the rainbow as a sign of his permanent commitment to this pledge (Gen 9:16). The oath and the sign in place, Noah fellowships with God through the symbolic ritual of sacrifice (Gen 8:20–22). A new relationship is born.

The covenant thus becomes God's mechanism for preserving his original plan. As he had done in the beginning, God separates the waters

---

1. Clines, *Theme of the Pentateuch*, 81.
2. Williamson, "Covenant," 139.

from the dry land (Gen 8:1; cf. Gen 1:9–10), initiates the repopulation of the earth (Gen 8:17–19; cf. Gen 1:20–22, 24–25), blesses humankind (Gen 9:1; cf. Gen 1:28), reestablishes days and seasons (Gen 8:22; cf. Gen 1:14–18), calls for humanity to again be fruitful and multiply (Gen 9:1, 7; cf. Gen 1:28), restores human responsibility over creation (Gen 9:2; cf. Gen 1:28), again provides food (Gen 9:3; cf. Gen 1:29–30), and reconfirms humanity's unique value as a creation in God's own image (Gen 9:6; cf. 1:26–27). Order, purpose, a calling, abundance, and blessing are the benefits of Noah's newfound covenant with God. There is a new beginning—albeit in the context of the still lingering effects of the fall.

God's covenant with Noah thus sets the stage for his future relations with both Israel and all of humanity. As Williamson observes, "the universal scope of this covenant implies that the blessing for which humanity was created and the creation that had been preserved through the flood will ultimately encompass not just one people or nation, but rather the whole earth."[3] Indeed, God never annuls his covenant with Noah as is evidenced both by the continuing sign of the rainbow and by the permanence expressed by God's language: "this is the sign of the covenant which I am making between me and you and every living creature that is with you, *for all successive generations*" (Gen 9:12). Rather than annul or supersede God's covenant with Noah, God's future covenants will continue to advance God's goal of creating relational intimacy with his people apart from sin in the environment of a newly created world.

As Scripture that is "profitable for teaching, for reproof, for correction, and for training in righteousness," the Noah story is a corrective to contemporary postures of tolerance toward all behaviors and lifestyles. Revisionist dismissal of God's wrath requires a radical alteration of Scripture and the utter breakdown of biblical theology. Deities of compromising tolerance may be popular in our contemporary world, but they do not accurately represent the God of the Bible. God's wrath resurfaces throughout the Bible until its consummation in the final judgment of Revelation 20.

But, again, there is a silver lining. As Scripture "profitable for teaching," the Noah account foreshadows Paul's later claim that where sin abounds God's grace hyper-abounds. For God's covenant with Noah promises hope for the future reconciliation of the nations, the creation of

3. Ibid., 141.

a new earth, and God's blessing of the nations—a promise that God extends in a special way to Abraham, the next recipient of God's covenantal plan.

"Father Abraham had many Sons, I am One of them and so are You!"

The occasion was Hogmanay 1990—the Scottish New Year's eve. The place was Nethy Bridge, a small village in the highlands of Scotland, where my wife, two brothers, and I had made a short excursion from Aberdeen. Late on that dark cold evening, we were enjoying the Scottish hospitality of our unsuspecting hosts in their cozy bed and breakfast. Suddenly, without warning, a troop of rambunctious but altogether good natured youths came "first footing" through the front door with their "right legs in" and their "left legs out." Three talented bagpipers burst forth booming with great animation, while the remaining voices rapturously sang *"Father Abraham had many sons, I am one of them and so are you!"* The cottage walls and every knickknack within shook from the frenzied exuberance and the booming bagpipes. Utterly stunned, our only option was surrender. Bursting into uncontrolled laughter, we joined the hilarious scene together with our nervous but welcoming hosts. An unforgettable time was had by all.

Whether or not composer Pierre Kartner intended it, the jingle *Father Abraham*[4] reminds us that Jews, Muslims, and Christians all trace their faiths back to the patriarch Abraham, whose story is told in the middle chapters of the book of Genesis: *Father Abraham had many sons, I am one of them and so are you.* Jews explain their identity as God's chosen people on the basis of God's promise to bring forth a chosen people from Abraham and Sarah's son, Isaac. Muslims revere Abraham as the ideal Muslim—a true monotheist and uncompromising opponent of idolatry. And Christians, following the theology of the apostle Paul, walk "in the footsteps" of Abraham's faith to inherit the covenant promises through Abraham's descendant Jesus (Romans 4; Galatians 3).

---

4. *Father Abraham* is a contemporary song composed by Pierre Kartner (b. 1935), a grandfatherly figure who himself goes by the alter ego, Father Abraham. Kartner's fame and fortune has not come as much from the famous song that rocked our Hogmanay but from the song he wrote in 1977 for the original Smurf's movie.

Covenants Establish Binding Relationships

The Secret of the Lord is for those who fear him,

And he will make them know his covenant.

(Ps 25:14)

George Mendenhall and Gary Heron define the ancient Near Eastern concept of covenant as "an agreement enacted between two parties in which one or both make promises under oath to perform or refrain from certain actions stipulated in advance."[5]

The goal of ancient Near Eastern covenants was the establishment of a mutually beneficial relationship that did not previously exist.

Appreciating the covenant institution, a common facet of ancient Near Eastern life, is essential to understanding biblical theology. It's a paradigm from the actual history and culture of the biblical world—not a system retrofitted anachronistically from a later theologian's desk. It's genuinely there and is true to the mindset of the biblical authors. As we shall see, the covenant is the nucleus around which the law, wrath, sacrifice, justification, and forgiveness function as orbiting satellites. The last-named simply cannot be understood without understanding the covenant.

The biblical word *covenant* refers to God's *pact* with Abraham and his descendants. God initiated the covenantal relationship, sometimes portrayed in Scripture as a marriage,[6] and established its mutual responsibilities. In response Abraham and his descendants accepted God's terms and committed themselves to fidelity to God and to his binding relationship with them. In return for God's protection and blessings, Abraham and his descendents were to devote themselves to God with undivided worship and to live with a conduct that reflected God's holy character. Both parties promised to be faithful to one another. As God's people, Israel was to be distinct from paganism, as God was distinct from pagan idols.

---

5. "Covenant," 1179. George Mendenhall was arguably last century's leading authority on the covenant. Professor Emeritus from the University of Michigan (1951–86), he served in the US Navy in WWII as a specialist deciphering Japanese codes before getting his PhD from Johns Hopkins University under the tutelage of the famous archaeologist and historian W. F. Albright.

6. Jer 31:32; Ezek 16:8, 32; Hos 2:19–20.

This simple concept is *the* major metaphor for understanding God's relationship to his people in the Bible. Without understanding it, one cannot understand the Bible. And so it is that the canon of the Christian Bible divides between the Old Testament (= Old Covenant) and the New Testament (= New Covenant), God's ultimate goal being intimate, holy relationship with his chief creation (Lev 19:2; 1 Pet 1:15–16).

The Features of the Covenant

Mendenhall and Heron list the following as recurring features of ancient Near Eastern covenants:

1. Identification of the Covenant Giver

2. Historical Prologue

3. Stipulations for the Covenant

4. Provisions for Deposit and Public Reading

5. List of Witnesses to the Treaty

6. Blessings and Curses

7. A Ratification Ceremony

8. Imposition of Curses

Parallels are unmistakable between these features of secular ancient Near Eastern covenants and Israel's covenant with God. Each feature finds a counterpart somewhere in Scripture.

1. *Identification of the Covenant Giver*: "I am the Lord who brought you out of Ur of the Chaldeans, to give you this land to possess it" (Gen 15:7); "I am God Almighty; walk before me, and be blameless. And I will establish my covenant between me and you, and will multiply you exceedingly" (Gen 17:1–2).

2. *Historical Prologue*: "I am the Lord *who brought you out of Ur of the Chaldeans*" (Gen 15:7); "I am the Lord your God, *who brought you out of the land of Egypt*" (Lev 26:13).

3. *Stipulations for the Covenant*: "walk before me and be blameless. And I will establish my covenant between me and you" (Gen 17:1–2).

4. *Provisions for Deposit and Public Reading*: "And these words, which I am commanding you today, shall be on your heart; and you shall teach them diligently to your sons and shall talk of them when you sit in your house and when you walk by the way and when you lie down and when you rise up. And you shall bind them as a sign on your hand and they shall be as frontals on your forehead. And you shall write them on the doorposts of your house and on your gates" (Deut 6:6–9).

The preceding verses of this, the first passage recited in traditional synagogue services of worship, affirms that Israel's original identity was not religious or legal by nature but entirely relational—"*Hear, O Israel! The Lord is our God, the Lord is one! And you shall love the Lord your God with all your heart and with all your soul and with all your might*" (Deut 6:4–5). This passage, equally prioritized by Jesus (Mark 12:29–30), reveals the wisdom that *God is a person* who desires intimate relationship with his people. Devoid of legalism, it speaks of passionate relationship: "*love*" ... "*with all your heart*" ... "*with all your soul*" ... "*with all your might.*"

5. *List of Witnesses to the Treaty*: God's divine witness to the covenant establishes the foundation for his future judgment. The Bible's omission of a list of divine witnesses is consistent with Israel's belief in one God (monotheism) and is therefore an expected deviation from the ancient Near Eastern norm. The people of Israel are themselves witnesses to the covenant: "And Joshua said to the people, 'You are witnesses against yourselves that you have chosen for yourselves the Lord, to serve him.' And they said, 'we are witnesses'" (Josh 24:22).

6. *Blessings and Curses*: "Now it shall be, if you will diligently obey the Lord your God, being careful to do all his commandments which I command you today, the Lord your God will set you high above all the nations of the earth. And all these blessings shall come upon you and overtake you, if you will obey the Lord your God" (Deut 28:1–2). "But it shall come about, if you will not obey the Lord your God, to observe to do all his commandments and his statutes with which I charge you today, that all these curses shall come upon you and overtake you" (Deut 28:15).

7. *A Ratification Ceremony*: The ratification ceremony involved two parts: first, the people committed verbally to obey the covenant—"all that the Lord has spoken we will do" (Exod 19:8; 24:3); second, they observed the

ritual of sacrifice, which reminded them of the just consequence of their sin, should they ever betray God. Like the sacrificial animal with which they were identifying, they would suffer the curse of death if they broke their covenant with God. The animal's life was given as a substitute for the individual sinner or for the community, so that life could continue with past sins accounted for by the sacrifice. The sacrifice paid the debt for sin.

This understanding of the covenant relationship is essential for comprehending the Christian concepts of sin and salvation. The apostle Paul, a Jewish Pharisee versed in covenant theology, would famously write that "the wages of sin is death" (Rom 6:23). Similarly, in John's Gospel, John the Baptist would promote Jesus as the solution to sin with the pronouncement: "Behold, the lamb of God who takes away the sin of the world" (John 1:29). Neither statement would make sense apart from the preexisting logic of the covenant.

This theological situation begs the question of God's relationship with the Gentile world. It is not in covenant with God like Israel, so why does the Gentile world incur death for breaking the covenant?

Paul anticipates this very question in Romans 1:18–32, where he appraises the sinful state of all humankind as being the consequence of the world's exchange of God for alternative objects of worship. All of humanity is as culpable as Israel for rejecting God in view of the fact that God in the beginning made his attributes and eternal power known to everyone through his creation. Despite this privilege, the Gentile world, like Israel, rejected God, so that they also are without excuse (Rom 1:20) and stand before God in a state of separation and sin. In separation from God, their plight is detachment from the eternal life source and thus inevitable death.

In the face of this situation, the gospel will announce God's continued love both for his covenant people and for the Gentile world (Rom 5:8, where both Jew and Gentile are in view). God's plan of salvation will afford Gentiles the opportunity to be grafted into the covenant blessings of Israel (Rom 11:17), so that once "the fullness of the Gentiles has come in . . . all Israel will be saved" (Rom 11:25b–26a).

But that is the subject of our next chapter. Having seen a preview of things to come, we must now return to the subject at hand.

Thus, as in secular ancient Near Eastern covenants, Israel's covenant with God presupposed that should Israel commit treason against her God and king, the consequence would be the death penalty. With this understanding, the prophet Isaiah rebuked Judah's idolatry warning that Judah, having forsaken God, now lived in a virtual covenant with death (Isa 28:15, 18). This corporate death would take the form of excessive military losses and eventual exile. Judah's separation from God would result in the loss of the covenantal blessings including the Promised Land.

8. *Imposition of Curses*: The Bible therefore interprets Israel's defeat and exile as God's enforcement of the covenant curse:

> And all the nations shall say, why has the Lord done thus to this land? Why this great outburst of anger. Then men shall say, because they forsook the covenant of the Lord, the God of their fathers, which he made with them when he brought them out of the land of Egypt. And they went and served other gods and worshiped them, gods whom they have not known and whom he had not allotted to them. Therefore, the anger of the Lord burned against that land, to bring upon it every curse which is written in this book (Deut 29:24–27).

The covenant thus established for God's people wise ways of thinking and wise norms for behavior. God effectively communicated his will to Abraham through the covenant language of Abraham's own culture. The simple message of the covenant was that the *security of Abraham's children was based entirely on faithful relationship with God—they were to be his people and he was to be their God.*

A strategic part of Scripture that gives wisdom that leads to salvation, the covenant defines salvation as a restoration of the relationship that was severed by Adam and Eve's treason. Salvation is a restored relationship with God made possible by God's action to restore a relationship previously broken.

For this reason the major analogies to God in the Bible are all relational. God is like a king who governs his people perfectly and justly. God is like a shepherd who cares for and protects his sheep. God is like a father who loves his people as his own children. God is like a husband, a covenant partner, who passionately loves his people as a jealous husband loves his bride. Even non-relational metaphors find their meaning in this relational background. God is not physically a rock, a fortress, or a hiding place, but God's person is the exclusive place where his people may find peace and security.

Genesis 17

Genesis 17 provides the contours of the covenant relationship and the rationale for understanding God's actions of judgment and deliverance throughout the Bible.

> Now when Abram was ninety-nine years old, the Lord appeared to Abram and said to him, "I am God Almighty; walk before me, and be blameless. And I will establish my covenant between me and you, and I will multiply you exceedingly." And Abram fell on his face, and God talked with him, saying, "As for me, behold, my covenant is with you, and you shall be the father of a multitude of nations. No longer shall your name be called Abram,[7] but your name shall be called Abraham;[8] for I will make you the father of a multitude of nations. And I will make you exceedingly fruitful, and I will make nations of you, and kings shall come forth from you. And I will establish my covenant between me and you and throughout their generations for an everlasting covenant, to be God to you and to your descendants after you" (Gen 17:1–7).

Covenant with Abraham was God's act of further reconciliation with sinful humanity. It revealed his action to see his original plan come to pass—he was not moving to a plan B but resurrecting plan A.

Why Abraham?

God's choice of Abraham does not relate to ethnic origin, religious observation, or moral purity. For prior to his encounter with God, Abram as he was then called, was just as pagan as everyone else. A descendant of Noah's son Shem—and thus a Semite—Abram came from the pagan land of Ur. From this background he would have been exposed to beliefs in many deities and worldviews that would later be rejected by his descendants, the Jews. Abraham was hardly a mythical character. To the contrary, the Bible portrays him as beset with human frailty. In one embarrassing episode, for instance, he displays moral cowardice when he passes Sarah, his wife, off as his sister, rather than risk his life to protect her from Pharaoh (Gen 12:11–19).

---

7. *Abram* = Hebrew for *"exalted father."*
8. *Abraham* = Hebrew for *"father of a multitude."*

And yet God chose this very man to be the forefather of his covenant people. Why?

For *one* simple reason—because of his *faith*. Genesis 15 tells the story. The word of God came in a vision: "Do not fear, Abram, I am a shield to you; your reward shall be very great" (Gen 15:1). This promise comes as a direct challenge to Abram's view of reality, which associated future security with male offspring. Abram was without a male heir.

He thus responded to God's promise in a state of confusion: "O Lord God, what will you give me, since I am childless, and the heir of my house is Eliezer of Damascus? . . . Since you have given no offspring to me, one born in my house is my heir" (Gen 15:2–3).

God then elevates the promise from ambiguity to what would have seemed to Abram as a pipe dream: "'This man will not be your heir; but one who shall come forth from your own body, he shall be your heir.' And he took him outside and said, 'Now look toward the heavens, and count the stars, if you are able to count them.' And he said to him, 'So shall your descendants be'" (Gen 15:4–5).

This promise required nothing short of a miracle because Abram's wife Sarah was old and barren. In modern terms, she was past menopause, and on top of that she hadn't had children even in her youth. For Sarah to have a child was simply impossible.

But that was God's covenant promise—the impossible. The language was not allegorical or figurative. It was literal and unequivocal. Abraham *would* have a son *through Sarah*. And characteristic of God, this promise would exceed what Abraham could ever imagine or think or count—his descendants would equal the number of stars in the sky.

Abraham believed this remarkable promise from God—and that's what mattered. He believed not as a consequence of theological reasoning or logical syllogism; he believed as a consequence of his direct encounter with God. He discovered the awesomeness of God through personal encounter.

Genesis describes Abram *falling on his face* when God talked to him. God's undeniable, overwhelming presence gave birth to Abraham's faith. In falling on his face, Abraham worshipped God in spirit and truth and humility. His faith emerged from the authentic act of falling on his face before the true living God—an intellectual act to be sure, but relational all the same (Gen 17:3). Abraham's faith emerged from a worshipful response to the reality of God.

It is critically important to chart exactly what Abraham believed, as his faith later becomes the prototype for the Christian faith that the apostle Paul claims as essential for the true people of God. As we have seen, Abraham believed that God, in bringing a child from Sarah's barren womb, could do the humanly impossible. As the creator of life in the beginning, God could give new life in the present. This is the critical connection between covenant and creation in biblical theology and between Abraham's justifying faith in Genesis and Paul's justifying faith in Romans. Both express belief in God's ability to do the impossible with particular respect to God's continued ability to create life. Abraham believed that God could bring forth a nation from his old decrepit body, and God reckoned his faith proactively as covenant righteousness (Gen 15:6). And so God prefigured later acts of salvation by bringing forth a son from Sarah's barren womb.

Paul, by comparison, calls upon his Roman audience to confess Jesus as Lord and believe that God raised Jesus from the dead—an analogous belief that God can do the impossible. The result Paul professes is that this faith too will be reckoned as covenant righteousness (Rom 10:10). That Paul intended the correlation is made plain by Rom 4:23–25: "Now not for his (Abraham's) sake only was it written, that it was reckoned to him, but for our sake also, to whom it will be reckoned, as those who believe in him who raised Jesus our Lord from the dead, he who was delivered up because of our transgressions, and was raised because of our justification." Paul's concept of salvation is therefore conceptually related to the covenant and contingent on God's continued power to create: "(as it is written, 'A father of many nations I have made you') *in the sight of him whom he believed, even God, who gives life to the dead and calls into being that which does not exist*" (Rom 4:17).

Abraham also believed that God could and would *bless* him beyond what he could imagine. He believed that God desired for him to have life and to have life abundantly. Not only would he have descendants, but they would be myriad—like the stars of the sky or the grains of sand on the seashore.

Still further, Abraham believed the truthfulness of God's word. Unlike Adam and Eve, Abraham trusted God and acted on his belief in God's word. Abraham's was not a leap of faith—an intellectual free fall—it was, as Paul described it, a *walk* of faith that all true believers share (Rom 4:12).

Abraham thus had a conversion experience in the truest sense. He *turned* from the pagan culture of his day to adopt a worldview governed by the reality of the one true God. He turned *from* paganism *to* God and adopted a totally new way of thinking.[9] In so doing, Abraham exemplified true repentance in both the Old Testament and New Testament senses of the word.

Upon this change appropriated by faith and made possible by God's unilateral action, Abraham entered an intimate relationship with the true creator God. He was restored to a relationship that had not existed since the fall of Adam and Eve—he was reckoned as *righteous* before God. "Then he believed in the Lord; and he reckoned it to him as righteousness" (Gen 15:6). The curse of the fall began to give way to the blessings of the covenant.

By covenant agreement, Abraham was now essentially "married" to God. His descendants through Sarah would be the people of God. And God would be their king.

On the basis of this relational understanding, the writers of Scripture consistently reiterate what is sometimes called the covenant formula: *"they shall be my people and I shall be their God."*[10] As Scripture that gives the wisdom that leads to salvation, the simple message of the covenant is that deliverance from the curse of the fall comes only through restored relationship with the one and only creator God. And this reconciliation has been made possible through God's action on behalf of fallen humanity. Reconciliation with God is possible on the basis of God's power exercised in miraculous *recreation*. God's doing of the impossible is a gift appropriated by faith.

The Mosaic Covenant

The words "law" and "commandment" are pejorative in contemporary society. They conjure up negative associations with other pejorative words like "legalistic," "strict," "oppressive," "intolerant," "narrow," "unforgiving," "uncompromising," and "constricting." Perhaps it is in part for this reason

---

9. The term *repentance* comes from the Hebrew word for *turn* in the Old Testament and the word for *change of mind* in the New Testament.

10. For a book length treatment of the covenant formula, see Rendtorff, *Covenant Formula*.

that the Ten Commandments play such a small role, if any, in Christian evangelism.

And yet imagine what the world would be like if everyone actually kept the Ten Commandments! A day of rest. Parents honored. No murder. No adultery. No stealing. No false witness. No envy. Wouldn't that be a better, freer, more liberating world?

We usually do not think of the Ten Commandments as part of a covenant, and yet Exodus defines the Ten Commandments expressly in covenant terms: "And he wrote on the tablets the words of the covenant, the Ten Commandments" (Exod 34:28). From the beginning, Exodus sets Moses' reception of the law (Exodus 20) firmly within the context of the Abrahamic covenant: "Now it came about in the course of those many days that the king of Egypt died. And the sons of Israel sighed because of the bondage, and they cried out; and their cry for help because of their bondage rose up to God. So God heard their groaning and God remembered his covenant with Abraham, Isaac, and Jacob (Exod 2:23–24; see also Exod 3:7–8, 16–22; 6:4–8; 13:5, 11; 33:1)."

Exodus tells the story of God's partial fulfillment of the Abrahamic covenant. When the story begins, the descendants of Abraham are a scattered people that number like the stars of the sky (Exod 1:7; Gen 12:2; 15:5). When Exodus ends, Israel is a unified nation ready to inherit Abraham's promised land. Along the way, in defeating Pharaoh, God curses "those who curse Abraham" (Gen 12:3) and keeps his side of the covenantal bargain. B. A. Anderson is thus able to conclude that "the Abrahamic covenant, which guarantees the promise of land and posterity, is the overarching theme within which the Mosaic covenant of law is embraced."[11]

The features of what is often called the "Mosaic covenant" can be found in Exodus 19–24. Prior to revealing the Ten Commandments, God explained to Moses the conditions upon which healthy covenant relations had to continue. The law thus became the covenant charter or constitution for God's relationship with his people. Anticipating Leviticus 19:2, the Israelites had to obey God and reflect his holy character. Their calling was to be a "kingdom of priests" and "a holy nation" that accurately represented God to the nations: "Now then, if you will indeed obey my voice and keep my covenant, then you shall be my own possession among all

---

11. Anderson, *Contours of Old Testament Theology*, 137.

the peoples, for all the earth is mine; and you shall be to me a kingdom of priests and a holy nation" (Exod 19:5–6).

The Ten Commandments revealed precisely how Israel was to be holy or set apart as God's covenant people. God was a holy God therefore his people had to set themselves apart by exhibiting God's original will for humanity through covenant fidelity (Exod 20:1–7), observing the covenant sign of rest (Exod 20:8–11), honoring parental authority (Exod 20:12), and maintaining moral purity (Exod 20:13–17). "Thus the primary concern of the Sinaitic covenant was on how the promised divine-human relationship between Yahweh and the 'great nation' descended from Abraham (Gen 17:7–8) should be expressed and maintained."[12]

The Ten Commandments were instructions for this path. They were not arbitrary laws but benevolent instructions. For Israel to reflect the character of her God, she had to be holy as her God was holy. To commit adultery, murder, steal, or bear false witness would be to adopt a character at odds with the holy, sinless character of God. And to break these commandments while maintaining identity as God's people would result in Israel's misrepresentation of God before the nations.

Remaining faithful to the covenant by keeping the law, Israel could become the blessing to the nations that God originally called them to be in his original encounter with Abraham (Gen 12:3). This call to holiness, a point of direct continuity between the Old Testament (Lev 19:2; 20:7) and the New (1 Pet 1:16; Matt 5:48), would never become obsolete.

Without dismissing each covenant's distinctive, we may thus say that the Mosaic law reveals in detail what the Abrahamic covenant communicated generally—namely, that God chose Abraham "in order that he may command his children and his household after him to keep the way of the Lord by doing righteousness and justice; in order that the Lord may bring upon Abraham what he has spoken about him" (Gen 18:19). Abraham's faith was fully expressed by his active obedience in keeping what he knew of God's law: "And I will multiply your descendants as the stars of heaven, and will give your descendants all these lands; and by your descendants all the nations of the earth shall be blessed; *because Abraham obeyed me and kept my charge, my commandments, my statutes and my laws*" (Gen 26:4–5).

12. Williamson, "Covenant," 150.

It is wrong therefore to see a dichotomy between faith and works or between faith and law—the Abrahamic a covenant of faith and the Mosaic a covenant of law. The Mosaic covenant is a revelation from the God of the Abrahamic covenant to the people of the Abrahamic covenant. By obeying God's voice and keeping his covenant (including the law), Moses' generation took up the call of becoming a kingdom of priests and a holy nation (Exod 19:5–6). The law is thus fully within God's comprehensive plan for salvation. It is with this conviction that the apostle Paul would clarify, "the law is holy, and the commandment is holy and righteous and good" (Rom 7:12).

The Davidic Covenant

No episode in Ken Taylor's *The Bible for Little Eyes* left a more indelible impression upon my "little eyes" than the depiction of David slaying Goliath. Goliath was terrifying. His gigantic frame, supersized armor, dark features, and frightening taunts left a haunting impression upon my young imagination.

Of course, the beastliness of Goliath only elevated the heroism of David's slingshot triumph. He was in the Bible what John Wayne was on TV.

Of course, I missed the theology entirely. Only much later would I realize that the story isn't as much about David as it is about God. The famous story is but one among many in the OT that witnesses God doing the humanly impossible to protect his covenant people and to bear evidence of his continued covenant loyalty. Young David's testimony is one of confidence in God alone:

> "For who is this uncircumcised Philistine, that he should taunt the armies of the living God?" (1 Sam 17:26).

> "The Lord who delivered me from the paw of the lion and from the paw of the bear, he will deliver me from the hand of the Philistine" (1 Sam 17:37).

> "This day the Lord will deliver you into my hands, and I will strike you down and remove your head from you. And I will give the dead bodies of the army of the Philistines this day to the birds of the sky and the wild beasts of the earth, that all the earth may know that there is a God in Israel, and that all this assembly may

know that the Lord does not deliver by sword or by spear; for the battle is the Lord's and he will give you into our hands" (1 Sam 17:46–47).

Within biblical theology this is more a story of David's faith and God's faithfulness than it is of David's heroic athleticism.

Ultimately, David's importance, like that of Noah, Abraham, Moses, and the writing prophets, is special because he is a recipient of a covenant promise from God. The Davidic Covenant, found in 2 Samuel 7:8–14 (1 Chr 17:2–15; Pss 2, 72, 89), is God's unconditional promise that he will raise up a descendant after David and establish his kingdom forever (2 Sam 7:12–13). This promise of God is the foundation for understanding the messianic promises of Isaiah, Jeremiah, and Ezekiel.

Matthew, Mark, and Luke each emphasize this connection as does the apostle Paul in the very first sentence of Romans. In fact, the entire New Testament closes with the risen Christ confirming his Davidic identity: "I am the root and the offspring of David, the bright morning star" (Rev 22:16).

Five major features of the Davidic covenant carry over from what has preceded and endure on to anticipate what will come in the future. First, the Davidic covenant is another faithful act of God's grace to preserve his people. The covenant is with David in particular, but 2 Samuel 7:8–11 presupposes that God will bless all of his people through the Davidic promise. Second, the Davidic covenant is an unconditional promise—God does not ask or demand anything of David—it is an act of grace. Third, the Davidic covenant is permanently binding and eternal in effect: "I will establish the throne of his kingdom *forever*" (2 Sam 7:14). The covenant thus has eschatological potential.[13] Trusting that God would not go back on his promise, successive generations of believing prophets would conserve the messianic hope upon this foundational promise. Fourth, the Davidic Covenant is intimately personal as it envisions a father/son relationship of faithfulness, rest, blessing, and permanent loving-kindness (2 Sam 7:15).

---

13. Eschatology has become complex in the study of theology. I use the word eschatology here simply in reference to revelations of the circumstances that will surround God's future action when he will bring history to an end in the resurrection of the dead, the final judgment, the creation of the new heavens and the new earth, and the afterlife. More than futurism, eschatology resonates with God's plans throughout history but focuses on the future completion of his eternal plan.

Fifth, it is originally in the context of the Davidic Covenant that God promises to build a house, the temple, for his name through the work of David's promised descendant (2 Sam 7:11, 13). Like God's covenants with Noah and Abraham, the Davidic Covenant had the long range goal of blessing the Gentile nations as well as the people of Israel (Ps 72:11; Isa 11:10). In the idyllic terms of Isa 11:1–9, this long-range plan conjoins the rule of the stem of Jesse (the Davidic heir) with the recreation of the earth and the restoration of paradise—"and the wolf will dwell with the lamb, and the leopard will lie down with the kid, and the calf and the young lion and the fatling together; and a little boy will lead them" (Isa 11:6). We may say that the long range goal of the Davidic covenant is once again the restoration of creation—the paradise lost by Adam and Eve's sin.

It is important to understand Jesus' title "Son of God" within this context. Son of God is not so much a title that discloses Jesus' divine supernatural identity as it is a messianic title that affirms Jesus' kingly fulfillment of the Davidic promise.[14] In this respect "Son of God," "Messiah," and "Christ" may be understood as nearly interchangeable terms in the New Testament, each referring to Jesus as God's *anointed* king over his covenant people.[15]

Like the Abrahamic, the Davidic covenant promises its recipient "a great name" (2 Sam 7:9; Gen 12:3), as befitting God's covenant partner. As with Abraham, this name will come with a victorious posterity (2 Sam 7:12–13, 16; Gen 17:5–8), including royal descendants (Gen 17:6). And like the Mosaic covenant, the Davidic covenant reflects the holy and just character of God by promoting God's justice and righteousness: "there will be no end to the increase of his government or of peace, on the throne of David and over his kingdom, to establish it and to uphold it with justice and righteousness from then on and forevermore. The zeal of the Lord will accomplish this" (Isa 9:7).

---

14. Jesus' divine lordship is implied more by his adoption of the title Son of Man, which traces back to the heavenly figure of Dan 7:13–14. It is interesting to note, however, that the title Son of Man also came to have messianic associations, as we know from Mark 14:61–62 and John 12:34 and extra-biblical texts such as *1 Enoch* 48:2–10 and *4 Ezra* 13:37, 52.

15. The terms *Messiah* and *Christ* both mean "anointed one." *Messiah* comes from Hebrew and *Christ* from Greek. As the heir of David who would rule on God's throne as his son, the Son of God figure in 2 Samuel 7 is a king and therefore an anointed figure as Ps 2:2 makes clear.

Thus, like its antecedents, the Davidic covenant, being permanently binding, instilled hope in each successive generation that believed in the eternal God of Israel who promised to be faithful, true, and unchanging. Though the Davidic covenant did not find immediate fulfillment in David's son, Solomon, or any other descendant during the era of the divided monarchies, God's past promise proved adequate in keeping alive the hope of a future coming messianic Son of God.

The New Covenant

Psalm 25:14 promises that "the secret of the Lord is for those who fear him, and he will make them know his covenant." This word of consolation and challenge reminds us that God's covenants are mysteries hidden from the faculties of humanity until God discloses them in his appointed time. The covenants are revelations of God's plans that originate exclusively in the mind of God who declares in Isaiah 55:9: "For as the heavens are higher than the earth, so are my ways higher than your ways, and my thoughts than your thoughts." When we come to the new covenant—as it is explicitly promised in Jeremiah 31:31–34 and dynamically portrayed in Isaiah, Ezekiel, Hosea, and Malachi—we encounter a fresh installment of God's mysterious covenant plan. In biblical contexts otherwise steeped in judgment, the new covenant promises amaze us with radically fresh insight into God's spectacular plans for the salvation of his people. God will do no less than exercise his creative power to *recreate* his people thereby accomplishing the humanly impossible in order to sustain his original plan.

It is this "mysterious" wisdom (1 Cor 2:7–8) that exhilarated the apostle Paul when he combined two new covenant passages in Isaiah to exclaim: "things which eye has not seen and ear has not heard, and which have not entered the heart of man, all that God has prepared for those who love him" (1 Cor 2:9; Isa 64:4; 65:17).

For the reader's convenience, we shall accumulate the features of the new covenant as they unfold in Jeremiah 31:31–34, and then add additional features as they appear in other related passages in the Old Testament. The synthesis that results will provide the essential DNA of new covenant (= New Testament) salvation.

> Behold, days are coming, declares the Lord, when I will make a
> new covenant with the house of Israel and with the house of Judah,

> not like the covenant which I made with their fathers in the day
> I took them by the hand to bring them out of the land of Egypt,
> my covenant which they broke, although I was a husband to them,
> declares the Lord. But this is the covenant which I will make with
> the house of Israel after those days, declares the Lord, I will put
> my law within them, and on their heart I will write it; and I will be
> their God, and they shall be my people. And they shall not teach
> again, each man his neighbor and each man his brother, saying,
> know the Lord, for they shall all know me, from the least of them
> to the greatest of them, declares the Lord, for I will forgive their
> iniquity, and their sin I will remember no more. (Jer 31:31–34; see
> also Jer 32:37–41)

This passage, explicitly quoted in Hebrews 8:8–12, reveals at least eight features of the new covenant:

1. The new covenant is a future hope that has not yet arrived in the time of the prophet—"behold days are coming." The new covenant is thus an eschatological hope.

2. The new covenant is made by God and as such is an expression of God's creative power exercised to save. In the same light, the new covenant will vindicate God among the nations, prove his holiness, and demonstrate that he is in fact Lord (cf. Ezek 36:22–23).

3. The new covenant is with the peoples of Israel and Judah. In this respect the new covenant exists in continuity with God's covenants with Abraham, Moses, and David. The conjoining of Israel and Judah signals God's plan for the reconciliation of his divided people, who had been estranged from one another since the death of Solomon. At the same time, the new covenant will bring with it an ingathering of God's people from their sin caused exiles in Assyria (722 BCE) and Babylon (586 BCE). This event is sometimes referred to in biblical theology as a "new exodus"—"For I will take you from the nations, gather you from all the lands, and bring you into your own land" (Ezek 36:24; cf. Isa 51:10–11).

4. The new covenant expresses the deep intimacy of God's passionate love for his people—"I was a husband to them." The description of the covenant as analogous to marriage finds detailed expansion in the new covenant expressions of Ezekiel 16, Hosea 1–3, and the language that begins Jeremiah 31: "I have loved you with an everlasting love; therefore I have drawn you with loving-kindness" (Jer 31:3).

5. The new covenant is new with respect to its *internal* nature. Whereas the Mosaic covenant was written on stone (Exod 24:12; 31:18), the new covenant is written on human hearts (Jer 31:33; 24:7; Ezek 36:26; cf. Rom 2:28; 2 Cor 3:2–3). It is in this internal respect that the new covenant is "not like" the old. At the same time, however, the new covenant does accomplish the goal of the Mosaic law by writing the *law* on the hearts of God's people. The new covenant thus perfects the law.

6. The new covenant maintains God's plan for relationship with his people: "and I will be their God, and they shall be my people" (Jer 31:33). Though a new installment, the new covenant remains within God's larger covenant plan. It, too, is a part of plan A.

7. The new covenant establishes a corporate blessing without discrimination: "they shall all know me from the least of them to the greatest" (Jer 31:34). In distributing the new covenant blessings, God will not show favoritism with respect to human reputation or economic profile.

8. The new covenant promises a future day of *forgiveness*: "for I will forgive their iniquity, and their sin I will remember no more" (Jer 31:34).

To these eight features of the new covenant, we now add ten more from related passages elsewhere in the Old Testament.

9. The new covenant will bring not only verbal forgiveness or acquittal from sin but also internal cleansing: "then I will sprinkle clean water on you, and you will be clean; I will cleanse you from all your filthiness and from all your idols" (Ezek 36:25).

10. The new covenant will bring a repentant spirit of contrition to the people of God. Forgiveness will not be superficial lip service but a genuine internal devotion. This is a particular emphasis of Ezekiel: "Thus I will establish my covenant with you, and you shall know that I am the Lord, in order that you may remember and be ashamed, and never open your mouth anymore because of your humiliation, when I have forgiven you for all that you have done, the Lord God declares" (Ezek 16:62–63; cf. Ezek 20:43; 36:31–32).

11. More than just cleansing, the new covenant will involve God's replacement of the hearts of his fallen people. The image is remarkably similar to that of a heart surgeon performing a modern day transplant: "Moreover, I will give you a new heart and put a new spirit within you; and I will remove the heart of stone from your flesh and give you a heart of flesh" (Ezek 36:26). Like a computer technician who replaces a virus infected obsolete system folder with a perfected new hard drive, so God promises to replace sin corrupted hearts with brand new perfectly functioning replacements. As creator, God will thus reverse the curses of Isaiah 6:9–10 with the saving measures of the new covenant.[16] This will involve both the writing of the law upon the heart and the pouring of the love of God into the hearts of believers through the indwelling of the Holy Spirit (Rom 5:5).

12. God will perform this new covenant work through the indwelling of the Holy Spirit on a *corporate* level: "And I will put my Spirit within you and cause you to walk in my statutes, and you will be careful to observe my ordinances. And you will live in the land that I gave to your forefathers; so you will be my people and I will be your God" (Ezek 36:27–28; cf. Isa 59:21).

13. As part of the larger eschatological hope, the new covenant will bring blessing to the nations, thereby fulfilling the Abrahamic covenant:

> And as for me, this is my covenant with them, says the Lord: my Spirit which is upon you, and my words which I have put in your mouth, shall not depart from your mouth, nor from the mouth of your offspring, nor from the mouth of your offspring's offspring, says the Lord, from now and forever. Arise, shine; for your light has come, and the glory of the Lord has risen upon you. For behold, darkness will cover the earth, and deep darkness the peoples; but the Lord will rise upon you, and his glory will appear upon you. And nations will come to your light, and kings to the brightness of your rising (Isa 59:21—60:3).

14. The new covenant will involve the fulfillment of the Davidic promises. In conjunction with the Holy Spirit, the Davidic heir will bring the new covenant promises to pass: "Behold, days are coming, declares the Lord, when I will fulfill the good word which I have spoken concerning the house of Israel and the house of Judah. In

16. See Meadors, *Idolatry and the Hardening of the Heart.*

those days and at that time I will cause a righteous Branch of David to spring forth; and he shall execute justice and righteousness on the earth" (Jer 33:14–15).

> And my servant David will be king over them, and they will all have one shepherd; and they will walk in my ordinances, and keep my statutes, and observe them. And they shall live on the land that I gave to Jacob my servant, in which your fathers lived; and they will live on it, they, and their sons, and their son's sons, forever; and David my servant shall be their prince forever. And I will make a covenant of peace with them; it will be an everlasting covenant with them. And I will place them and multiply them, and will set my sanctuary in their midst forever. My dwelling place also will be with them; and I will be their God, and they will be my people (Ezek 37:24–27; cf. Ezek 34:23–24).

Thus, the new covenant will fulfill the Davidic promises.

15. The new covenant is everlasting and unconditional (Jer 32:37–41; 50:5). Building on the faith that God does not change and is true to his word, the new covenant is a stimulus for hope in God's love, forgiveness, and re-creative power. The new covenant thus reinvigorates hope in God.

16. Yet the new covenant will involve the refinement of God's people through suffering: "And I will bring the third part through the fire, refine them as silver is refined, and test them as gold is tested. They will call on my name, and I will answer them, I will say, 'they are my people,' and they will say, 'the Lord is my God'" (Zech 13:9). The new covenant thus involves the discipline of God's people and the refinement of their character into conformity with God's nature (cf. Gal 4:19).

17. In conjunction with the new exodus theme, the new covenant will entail the restoration and glorification of Jerusalem, often referred to with the eschatological name Zion: "And they shall come and shout for joy on the height of Zion, and they shall be radiant over the bounty of the Lord" (Jer 31:12; cf. Jer 31:1–6; Isa 52:1–8). The symbolism is likely a reference to the establishment of God's absolute rule, as Jerusalem was conceived to be the place of God's throne. The restoration of Jerusalem would come with the arrival of the kingdom of God (Rev 21:10–21).

18. The new covenant prefigures the resurrection of the dead. "Then you will know that I am the Lord, when I have opened your graves and caused you to come up out of your graves, my people. And I will put my Spirit within you, and you will come to life, and I will place you on your own land. Then you will know that I, the Lord, have spoken and done it, declares the Lord" (Ezek 37:13–14). Drawn from Ezekiel's vision of the valley of dry bones, this disclosure depicts God breathing back into existence a united Israel that God's servant David will govern forever. The literal fulfillment of this figurative language will require a fresh work of God's creative power.

Synthesizing these eighteen points—possibly more could be added—we may conclude that the new covenant reinvigorates hope in God by envisioning the fulfillment of previous promises and the revolutionary addition of new ones.

Putting it all Together: Creation, Sin, and Covenant

The covenants of the Old Testament build upon one another in revealing God's plan for the restoration of his people and for the restoration of creation. This is what theologians refer to as progressive revelation. One covenant does not replace another but rather expands its antecedents and furthers God's commitment through heretofore unexpected promises whose fulfillment only God can accomplish. The covenants thus require faith that God will remember his everlasting promises and bring them to pass in his appointed time. In initiating the new covenant God is emphatic that he has not forgotten the old: "Thus says the Lord, if my covenant for day and night stand not, and the fixed patterns of heaven and earth I have not established, then I would reject the descendants of Jacob and David my servant, not taking from his descendants rulers over the descendants of Abraham, Isaac, and Jacob. But I will restore their fortunes and will have mercy on them" (Jer 33:25–26; cf. Isa 51:1–3).

The old promises are thus still binding. The law will authenticate God's new covenant people *internally* as it is to be written upon human hearts. God's people will live out the *Shema* (Deut 6:4–9) and the Ten Commandments not out of legalism but out of internal devotion and love.

It is evident that biblical generations saw the interrelationships of the covenants and the contributions they each made to the larger plan of

God. One need look no farther than Matthew 1:1 to see the synthesis and compatibility of the Abrahamic and Davidic covenants: "Jesus Christ, the son of David, the son of Abraham." Paul likewise synthesizes the respective covenant promises within his single concept of the gospel—the Davidic (Rom 1:1–3) merges with the Abrahamic (Romans 4; Galatians 3) and the new (2 Cor 3:6; Rom 2:29) within argumentation that maintains the holiness, the goodness, and the righteousness of the law (Rom 7:12).

Continuity among the covenants finds further affirmation in the covenant formula "I will be their God and they will be my people," which relates closely to God's revelation of himself as Lord. This formula articulates the purpose of the Abrahamic covenant (Gen 17:7–8), the Mosaic covenant (Exod 6:7; 29:45), the Davidic covenant (2 Sam 7:24), and the new covenant (Jer 31:33; Ezek 36:28; 37:27; Zech 8:7–8) before assuming a prominent role in Paul's identification of the true people of God (2 Cor 6:16–18). Then, finally, the covenant formula is front and center in Revelation's vision of eschatological salvation (Rev 21:3, 7). Continuity among the covenants is manifest.

In closing this chapter, we are now able to describe a coherent biblical theology that sets the stage for the coming of Christ and God's gift of salvation. God's ability to create is the premise for believing in his ability to accomplish a salvation that requires nothing less than the re-creation of the human heart and the resurrection of the dead. Sin has resulted in the breaking of the covenant and the affliction of the covenant curses including separation from God, hardening, and death. The covenants, being unconditional and everlasting, promise the hope and means of forgiveness, reconciliation, healing, and new birth through the ministries of the Holy Spirit and the coming Davidic Messiah. Each contributes to the revelation of God's love and grace as he works toward an atoning relationship with his fallen people. As we shall see, it was Jesus' goal to accomplish this new covenant salvation, and it was Paul's call to proclaim it. It is to this matchless subject that we now turn.

Questions for Discussion, Further Study, and Meditation

- In your own words, define the major features of the covenant institution.

- Why is it appropriate to refer to the Bible as comprised of the Old Testament (= Old Covenant) and the New Testament (= New Covenant)? How does the Old relate to the New?

- How would you describe the relationships among the covenants of Noah, Abraham, Moses, David, and the new covenant as prophesied by Isaiah, Jeremiah, Ezekiel, and Hosea?

- In what ways is it helpful to think of God's covenant with his people as being like a marriage? How might understanding of the covenant idea serve as a corrective to contemporary marital breakdown?

- Beyond marriage, how else might contemporary culture benefit from the instruction of covenantal ideals?

- What is the relationship between the biblical doctrines of creation, sin, and covenant?

Suggested Scripture Reading

Genesis 12, 15, 17, 26–28; Exodus 2, 20, 24, 31; Isaiah 54; Jeremiah 31; Ezekiel 36; Hosea 2; Matthew 1:1–17; Luke 1–2, 22:20; Romans 4; 2 Corinthians 3; Galatians 3–4; Hebrews 7–10; Revelation 19–20.

4

Salvation: What God Made, He can Fix

For God so loved the world, that he gave his only begotten Son, that whoever believes in him should not perish, but have everlasting life."

(John 3:16–17)

Briskly turning the corner of a dark street in Thessaloniki, Greece, my eyes chanced upon the solitary reference 3:16. It was embroidered in white against the black background of a baseball cap worn by a middle aged Greek pedestrian—a strange sight on any continent but especially so in the culture of Greek Orthodoxy. Odd though it was, the hat served its purpose well. Instantly my mind processed the famous words. And after a brief mental pause, I walked on contemplating the profound message of John 3:16. Is it really true?

Wikipedia identifies John 3:16 as "one of the most widely quoted verses from the Christian Bible. It has been called the 'gospel in a nutshell' because it is considered a summary of some of the most central doctrines of traditional Christianity." And so it is. No other verse in the Bible is quoted, preached, taught, or displayed quite like John 3:16. Indeed, as I found on that dark street corner in Thessaloniki, 3:16 speaks for itself like no other reference in world literature. Nothing even comes close.

Why? Perhaps because John 3:16 takes us further in addressing the numbing theological question we addressed in chapter 1: "*Who are we that God should take thought of us?*" (Ps 8:4). If God really is God in the orthodox Christian sense—that is, if he really is everywhere, all-knowing, all-powerful, eternal, and infinite—why would he stoop to find interest in the welfare of miniscule, here today and gone tomorrow humanity?

As my kids head off to college, time is suddenly of essence with respect to these big questions. Not just days and years, but it seems like decades are flying by. A lifespan suddenly seems short. How could the God *of eternity* find interest in the fleeting lives of human beings, whom the Bible describes as like grass which withers and fades away? Do our lives really matter? Or is agnostic Bible scholar Bart Ehrman correct when he identifies Ecclesiastes as the only true-to-life biblical worldview— "all is vanity and striving after wind."[1] If such is true and we're really not that important, does it really matter *what we believe*? Does it really matter *how we live*? Since we're all going to die anyway, *do our actions in history really matter*?

How one answers these questions will depend, ultimately, upon one's response to Genesis 1. To be sure, human beings conceivably may do good and meaningful things in the absence of God, but these good things do not have any kind of permanent value. We may advance technology, but that technology will become obsolete and eventually useless. We may foster education, but that education will eventually be forgotten. We may provide food and medicine and even love, but those we "rescue" will eventually suffer and die nonetheless. And then, we too will die—irrespective of our faith and deeds. And finally, if this is all there is, the human race will itself become extinct and human history will be deleted from reality, as if it never happened. For who will be there to say that it did happen?

These existential questions find their answers either in God, in nothing, or in fanciful science fiction. The biblical worldview, Ecclesiastes included, finds its answer in God's creative plan: "The conclusion, when all has been heard, is: fear God and keep his commandments, because this applies to every person. For God will bring every act to judgment, everything which is hidden, whether it is good or evil" (Eccl 12:13–14).

"No," the Bible answers, "reality will not delete the history of the human race, because God will survive history to judge what we have said and done." Yes, all of the above does matter—it matters what we think; it matters what we believe; it matters what we do. We really are important, because God has created us, he has initiated covenant with us, he

1. Ehrman, *God's Problem*, 159–96.

has sacrificed for us, and he will eventually judge us and determine our eternal fates. We are not mere blips on the radar screen of time and space, because we are fearfully and wonderfully made, and we have potential for eternal life. We are *persons* created in the image of God, who have the capacity for analytical thought and creativity. We can get our brains around the bigger physical realities of cars and buildings and airplanes and even solar systems. More impressively, we can think about the deep realities of abstract truth. We are bigger than time and space, because we can communicate and love in responsible, deeply meaningful relationships. We are persons, not objects. We have personality, a conscience, feelings, a will, and a soul. These capacities set us apart from time, space, matter, and the lower life forms. To one another and to God, we are more than inanimate carbon. Emotion, conscience, and innate justice signal the truth that there's more to reality than matter. We are created in God's image, we can live in covenant with him, and we are important. Remarkably, as John 3:16 reveals, God, the supreme power of the universe, the creator of time and space, *loves* us.

Salvation, in the gospel sense, begins with this revelation of God's loving character. God's love explains the new creation, Jesus' sacrifice, the forgiveness of sins, the new covenant, the possibility of being born again, the gift of the Holy Spirit, and the gift of eternal life. God, the Bible reveals, loves us more than a devoted, compassionate parent loves their child.

How so? Because God created us in the beginning and God wills to recreate us in the end. We are his. Since God desires to forgive, heal, and recreate us, things that no human parent can accomplish, we may rightly say that his love extends further than the reach of the most loving parents. This reality sets God apart as our heavenly Father. His love, the supreme power of the universe, alone is able to reverse the pain of suffering and the finality of death. And this is the very thing God wills to do in the lives of those who love him and believe in him with their lives. In his sovereign, all powerful love, God has acted to provide the opportunity and means for human beings to be *recreated*. As the God who created in the beginning, he still has the power to recreate both now and in the future. John 3:16 tells us that God wills to do just that because he genuinely loves us. He created us once. He can do it again—not a pipe dream but a very believable reality. What he created in the beginning, he can fix.

The desire of God is the restoration of his loving relationship with fallen humanity. The covenant has revealed to us that story. God desires for the actualization of the *Shema*—that we love him with all of our heart, soul, mind, and strength. A major feature of salvation is that God himself has acted to give us the capacity for such love: "hope does not disappoint, because *the love of God has been poured out within our hearts through his Holy Spirit* who was given to us" (Rom 5:5). Salvation is thus a relationship of love between a loving God and a newly created people of genuine love. Like marriage, covenant with God succeeds on the basis of responsible faithful eternal love. God's love is the *raison d'être* of salvation.

It is in relationship with God that ultimate security is found for the believer: "God causes all things to work together for good to those *who love God*" (Rom 8:28); "neither death, nor life, nor angels, nor principalities, nor things present, nor things to come, nor powers, nor height, nor depth, nor any other created thing, shall be able to separate us from *the love of God*, which is in Christ Jesus our Lord" (Rom 8:38–39). Rather than a health and wealth gospel based on a purely intellectual profession of faith, salvation is a living relationship of mutual love between living persons. The relationship does not entail separation from the realities of world suffering but engenders hope for the future and spiritual comfort in the present. Suffering is painful and real, but it is part of a bigger reality. And, as we have seen, it is not an unexpected shock for the biblically informed; it is the consequence of living in a broken Humpty Dumpty world.

Yet comprehensive reality does not begin or end with Humpty Dumpty's crash. For before the crash there was a sinless pure world perfectly created according to God's design. And on the other side of the crash there is hope in a world where the loving, forever faithful Creator still reigns. The gospel is God's revelation of his continued, all powerful love: "*And we have come to know and have believed the love which God has for us. God is love, and the one who abides in love abides in God, and God abides in him*" (1 John 4:16).

It is noteworthy that the two most revered passages of the Hebrew Scriptures, the Ten Commandments and the *Shema*, both emphasize the human responsibility to love God: "to those who love me and keep my commandments" (Exod 20:6); "You shall love the Lord your God with all your heart and with all your soul and with all your might" (Deut 6:4–5).

This love is a stark contrast to contemporary Harlequin Romances, which are entirely out of touch with reality. It is also a stark contrast to the romantic love of classical literature, where romantic love often ends in tragedy as famously depicted in Shakespeare's *Romeo and Juliet*. As we discovered in chapter 3, covenant love in the Old Testament does have emotional dimensions, but the spiritual passion of covenant expresses itself in responsible fidelity that perseveres through the stark realities of human life. The *Shema* therefore affirms that true covenant love is a comprehensive response from a person's entire being, not just their emotions or intellects—"*with all your heart, with all your soul, and with all your might.*"

At the end of the day, it will be love that matters most. Scottish geologist, explorer, and evangelist Henry Drummond (1851–97) reminds us of this forgotten biblical truth in his timeless classic *The Greatest Thing in the World*:

> In the book of Matthew, where the Judgment Day is depicted for us in the imagery of One seated upon a throne and dividing the sheep from the goats, the test of a man then is not, "How have I believed?" but "How have I loved?" . . . Sins of commission in that awful indictment are not even referred to. By what we have not done, *by sins of omission*, we are judged. It could not be otherwise. For the withholding of love is the negation of the Spirit of Christ, the proof that we never knew him, that for us he lived in vain. It meant that he suggested nothing in all our thoughts, that he inspired nothing in all our lives, that we were not once near enough to him to be seized with the fervency of his compassion for the world.[2]

Drummond's point is well taken. The deeds God approves bear testimony of the inner Christ-like love and faith of the authentic believer. As the apostle Paul put it so elegantly, "if I give all my possessions to feed the poor, and if I deliver my body to be burned, but do not have love, it profits me nothing" (1 Cor 13:3).

The Bible's teaching on love is indeed a teaching that gives wisdom that leads to salvation in Christ Jesus. It is a scriptural truth that those who *truly* love God love others as God has loved them. The parable in

---

2. Drummond, *Greatest Thing in the World*, 57–58. Like McDonalds' hamburgers, it's impossible to know how many copies of *Greatest Thing in the World* have been sold—over 12 million for sure since Dwight L. Moody first published the treatise on "the love chapter" (1 Corinthians 13) in 1884.

Matthew that Drummond alludes to thus concludes, "Then they them-selves also will answer, saying, 'Lord, when did we see you hungry, or thirsty, or a stranger, or naked, or sick, or in prison, and did not take care of you? Then he will answer them, saying, 'Truly I say to you, to the extent that you did not do it to one of the least of these, you did not do it to me'" (Matt 25:44–45). Elsewhere we find the same sentiment in 1 John 4:20–21: "If someone says, 'I love God,' and hates his brother, he is a liar; for the one who does not love his brother whom he has seen, cannot love God whom he has not seen. And this commandment we have from him, that the one who loves God should love his brother also."

New Creation: The New Heavens and the New Earth

Some take John 3:16 as referring to God's love for the physical world—the world of nature. But as biblical as God's love for his whole physical creation is, that is not the message of John 3:16. In John 3:16 the word *world* (*cosmos*) refers to the world of *fallen humanity*, as the reference to belief requires—the natural world is incapable of belief. This becomes clear upon a reading of John 7:7: "The *world* (*cosmos*) cannot hate you; but it hates me because I testify of it, that its deeds are evil." Clearly, Jesus is referring here to *people* and not the rest of the physical universe.

However, the Bible's concept of salvation does extend to the natural world. Christians should be alarmed at environmental apathy and capi-talistic recklessness, even if John 3:16 is the wrong text for making the point. Doesn't it make sense that God might value the beautiful world that he created? And, going a step further, is it not reasonable to think that the creator God will not only resurrect those who believe in him, but also recreate the polluted earth, so that he might fulfill his original plan?

Such in fact is the message of biblical salvation. Tied to the biblical hope for human salvation is the expectation of the restoration of the rest of the natural world: "For the anxious longing of the creation waits ea-gerly for the revealing of the sons of God. For the creation was subjected to futility, not of its own will, but because of him who subjected it, in hope that the creation itself also will be set free from its slavery to corruption into the freedom of the glory of the children of God. For we know that the whole creation groans and suffers the pains of childbirth together until now" (Rom 8:19–22).

How is this salvation of the natural world to take place? We, of course, do not know—other than that God himself will do it. Just as Genesis did not reveal the scientific procedures of creation, so also the Bible does not reveal scientific procedures relating to *re*creation. But, in the prophecy of Isaiah, and then again in the second to last chapter of the Bible, we do receive the promise that it will indeed take place: "For behold, I create new heavens and a new earth; and the former things shall not be remembered or come to mind" (Isa 65:17); "And I saw a new heaven and a new earth; for the first heaven and the first earth passed away, and there is no longer any sea" (Rev 21:1).

The biblical message is that God will act in the future to restore the fallen universe to his original design. Cleansing and restoration find expression in the symbolic statement that there will no longer be any sea (a symbol for the domain of evil in the ancient world). The message is that God will eliminate the sea/evil from his newly created universe. As it was in the beginning before the fall of Adam and Eve, so it shall be again in the new heavens and the new earth—a pure and clean physical universe without the contaminating effects of the fall. Theologically, therefore, an unfortunate disconnect exists in the thinking of contemporary Christians who dismiss the importance of stewardship of the environment. In the Bible, salvation is a both/and equation—God will save both his lesser creation, the physical earth, and his chief creation, whom he created in his own image.

This message about the future is scriptural in purpose—it has as its purpose the giving of wisdom that leads to salvation in Christ Jesus. It is not primarily about dates, codes, maps, and sensational predictions. The simple message is that those who persevere in faith now will enjoy the benefits of new life in the newly created universe in the future. Such is God's will. The paradise that was lost as a consequence of Adam and Eve's sin will be made possible once more in the future to those who exercise persevering faith now. Revelation, the Bible's final book, is a call to this wisdom that leads to eternal salvation: "He who overcomes shall inherit these things, and I will be his God and he will be my son" (Rev 21:7).

Forgiveness of Sins: The Sacrifice of Jesus Christ on the Cross

But God demonstrates his own love toward us, in that while we were yet sinners, Christ died for us (Rom 5:8).

For many intellectuals the cross is an insane symbol of gore and malicious torture. Why would a loving God send his son to suffer crucifixion as a bloody sacrifice for sin? It's ridiculous! If he really is omniscient and loving, why didn't God design a more comfortable, more palatable way of salvation? And if he really is omnipotent, why didn't God decree salvation by fiat? Why did Jesus have to suffer and die?

These questions lead us to the clarification that the God of the Bible is entirely different from the idealized god of postmodern culture. Academically safe religion bristles at the thought that God could be anything other than unconditionally tolerant and unconditionally permissive; that God could seriously care about sin; that God could really care about punishing injustice; that God could really have a plan for judging human beings for the things they have done.

The God of the Bible is very different, however; he cares on every front. What the apostle Paul said of his generation remains true for ours: "*All* have sinned and fallen short of the glory of God" (Rom 3:23). That *all* includes the author of this book. It includes people with short hair cuts, nice clothes, and good jobs. It includes people with Ivy League educations, who eat at nice places. It includes religious people of all faiths and political parties. It includes the fashionably contemporary worshiper and the conservative traditionalist. It includes all races, ethnic groups, and genders. It includes every socio-economic group. *All* have sinned and fallen short of the glory of God. *Such is the reality of our real world.* The cross is about the facts, not make believe.

That said, in being against sin the gospel is *not* against fun; it is not counter-pop-cultural or counter youthful exuberance. To the contrary, Christianity celebrates all creative expressions as cultivations of the creativity God originally instilled within humankind.

Christianity, however, does supersede pop culture by providing what pop culture can't—the cultivation of a *permanently* satisfying relationship (*culture* derives from the Latin word *cultus* = cultivate). As we are painfully aware, when left to its own devices, pop culture produces pop relationships. Like Coca Cola, pop relationships fizz at first before going flat and altogether undesirable. Sadly, pop culture is infamous for its shallow broken relationships—perennial fodder for tabloids, the paparazzi, and talk show slime. Behind the cosmetic veneer of Hollywood's celebrity idols exists a legacy of relational dysfunction—Marilyn Monroe, Elvis Presley, Michael Jackson, Elizabeth Taylor—icons whose fates belie the hollow reality of pop culture, where covenant is an unknown commodity. Much of pop culture lives in the suspended world of teen idolatry where wisdom and truth equate with boredom and where love is a feeling. Image and a "catchy beat" are everything.

Into this all too familiar arena, the Christian gospel enters with the refreshing offer of agape love—a responsible, enduring love that will consummate, ironically, in a lavish party complemented by the finest refined aged wine (Isa 25:6–9). Whereas pop relationships are like fizzy sugar water that goes flat, true covenant relationship is like a fine wine that gets better and better with age—excellent now but extraordinary tomorrow. The covenant cultivates an eternal relationship of mutually exhilarating agape love. The beat, the catchy words, the energetic fun—it's all fine and wonderful for the moment—but it's not enough, as we all discover with time and experience. The Coca Cola diet doesn't satisfy for long. This is because time moves on and death is real. Elvis *doesn't really live*. His corpse is six feet under, stone cold dead, and well on in the process of decay. The same is true for Marilyn and Michael. Money and image just don't matter. Ted Turner and Bill Gates are aging and will die just like the wandering refugees of Sudan.

According to the Bible, aging and death are universal realities because death is the universal consequence of sin—"the wages of sin is death" (Rom 6:23). It is a cancer everyone inherits at birth and everyone surrenders to in the end. It is reality. This cancer no one beats—ever.

As we observed in chapter 3, the ancient Jews contemplated this reality in their observance of sacrifice. When they broke their covenant with God, God provided sacrifice as a means by which an animal might serve as a substitute for the sinner. *The animal died in the place of the guilty sinner*. For the duration of the sacrificial system, this ritual made possible the continuation of God's relationship with his people despite their sinful violations of the covenant. Most importantly, the Jews never forgot that death alone was the expected punishment for the breaking of their covenant with God (see Jer 34:15–20). If he so desired, God would be justified in wiping them off the earth. It was purely by his grace that he kept Israel around.

It is against this background that the cross must be understood. If God really is God in the full biblical sense, he cannot have pure relationship with people whose sins still fester. For God's love is *holy* love. Sin is perverted. God's love is *just* and *righteous*. Sin is *unjust* and *unrighteous*.

God's love is a *responsible, righteous, re-creative* love that will settle for nothing but the *highest* good for his covenant partner. Sin, by comparison, is irresponsible, unrighteous, destructive, compromising, and ultimately self-seeking—altogether antithetic to God's covenant ideals.

God's will for the highest good is for sinners to become sinless—to be holy as God is holy. He desires that his people be entirely without the cancer of sin and as a result free from the effects of suffering and death. Jesus' elimination of sin and death thus aims to restore intimate pure relationship between God and humankind, which was God's original intent for creation and his guiding purpose for the covenant. It was for this that Jesus prayed in John 17:22–23: "And the glory which you have given me I have given to them; that they may be one, just as we are one; I in them, and you in me, that they may be perfected in unity, that the world may know that you sent me, and you love them, even as you have loved me."

God desires that his people be *one* with him. And that is impossible as long as sin remains in the picture. Because God is sinless—"in him there is no sin" (1 John 3:5)—his uncompromising standard for relationship is sinless, mutual faithfulness. His people *must* be holy as he is holy (Lev 19:2; 1 Pet 1:16) in order for atonement to occur and for humanity's highest interest to be realized. God's desire is for this very thing—the restoration of the sinless relationship that existed before Adam and Eve's disobedience.

The biblical authors thus compare the atonement to marriage—"for your husband is your maker, whose name is the Lord of hosts" (Isa 54:5; see also Hos 2:19–20; Jer 31:32–34). As a man leaves his father and mother to become one flesh with his wife, so do human beings leave their former lives to become one with God: "But the one who joins himself to the Lord is one spirit with him" (1 Cor 6:17).

God does not desire divorce or separation or a "look the other way" marriage of convenience. He does not have a plan B. As James Denny put it over a century ago, "The very glory of the atonement was that it manifested the righteousness of God; it demonstrated God's consistency with his own character, which would have been violated alike by indifference to sinners and by indifference to that universal moral order—that law of God—in which alone eternal life is possible."[3]

---

3. Denny, *Atonement and the Modern Mind*, 75–76.

The salvation Jesus speaks of is one prepared "from the foundation of the world" (Matt 25:34). In keeping with his original design for humanity, God wants relationship characterized by undivided passionate love and absolute faithfulness. Jesus' ministry thus fulfills Moses' promotion of the Shema as the most important law (Mark 12:29–30).

To go a step further, the purpose of Jesus' ministry was to create a new relationship between God and humanity through Jesus' *perfect* sacrifice. Fully God and fully man, Jesus became like us in order that we might become like him—sinless, holy, and eternal. As Paul informs us, Jesus acted as a mediator: "For there is one God, and one mediator also between God and men, the man Christ Jesus, who gave himself as a ransom for all" (1 Tim 2:5–6). Jesus' death on the cross was a fully human and yet fully divine sacrifice that effectively paid the price for humankind's sin. Jesus, as John the Baptist declared, was "the Lamb of God who takes away the sin of the world" (John 1:29). By the grace of God, he tasted death for everyone (Heb 2:9).

This message is not to be equated with bloody child sacrifice or infanticide. Rather, it is the message of Jesus' *volitional* sacrifice performed out of love for God and faithful obedience to God's plan for salvation—*he gave himself* as a ransom for all. This is a message of love, obedience, and faithfulness: "For this reason the Father loves me, because I lay down my life that I may take it again. No one has taken it away from me, but I lay it down on my own initiative" (John 10:18).

To be sure, Jesus' crucifixion was not an expression of cheap grace. It was a painful sacrifice. Saving faith does not follow cheap lip service to a creed or a nod toward an intellectual statement of assent or a social identification with a particular subculture. It is most definitely not a political affiliation. Saving faith involves union with the person, death, resurrection, and continued life of Jesus Christ. That is what it means to be "in Christ" and "with Christ."

Faith

On my tenth birthday, my parents surprised me with a miniature Sony radio. I was ecstatic—not for the Sony brand or the design or anything like that—and I could not have cared less about music, the weather, or the news. I *needed* a radio for one purpose. I was a fanatical St. Louis Cardinals baseball fan. Through static, rain delays, and the fading in and out of radio waves, I listened to Jack Buck and Mike Shannon give the Cardinals' play by play almost every KMOX broadcast.

My love for the Cardinals was vicarious. When the Budweiser ads subsided, I was not a ten year old listening from hundreds of miles away in Memphis, Tennessee; I was a bona fide member of the St. Louis Cardinals. When the Cardinals won, I won. When they lost, I suffered foul moods and shattered emotions—one extra innings loss to Willie Stargell and the Pirates threw me into a ballistic fit of rage that came ever so close to resulting in a spanking—my parents just didn't understand.

I didn't think of it this way then, of course, but my relationship with the Cardinals, in addition to being personal and passionate, was both corporate and individual. I identified with the whole team and its franchise corporately. I was by identity a St. Louis Cardinal. The Cardinals were my team. But at the same time, when the game started and my imagination took over, I was one specific player. I was an individual member of the Cards. For I identified individually with my hero—the Hall of Fame base stealer, Lou Brock. When Lou came up to bat, I came up to bat—slightly nervous with my pulse quickened and my adrenaline pumped. When Lou stole a base, I stole a base. His batting average was my batting average. When Lou didn't win the National League MVP award, I was robbed. Lou's reputation was my reputation.

On a much, much deeper level, an analogous phenomenon helps explain one dimension of Christian salvation through Jesus' death, burial, and resurrection. God's love for us is such that whereas I became one with the world of the St. Louis Cardinals, God in the person of Jesus Christ became one with the world of fallen humanity. Remarkably, Jesus identified with us—he did so corporately by identifying with all humanity, and he did so individually by identifying with each and every one. As God's replacement for Adam, Jesus represented all of Adam's descendents in his death for the justification of the broken covenant. Jesus vicariously identified with fallen humanity by taking on a physical body and experiencing temptation as we do and yet without sin (Heb 4:15). He took us to the cross when he vicariously substituted for our sin (Phil 2:5–11). His death paid the wage for our sin because he was one with us. As a king represents his people, so did Jesus represent us on the cross. In so doing, he defined love.

Jesus' death, however, does not guarantee universal salvation. John 3:16 does not say that "God so loved the world that he gave his only begotten son so that everyone will have eternal life." John 3:16 says, rather, "*whoever believes* in him will not perish but have eternal life." Salvation is appropriated through faith.

Why?

Faith is essential because it is the bonding agent that unites us with Christ, so that we vicariously become one with him in the events he performed once and for all for our salvation. Faith nails us to the cross with Christ. He identified with us through the incarnation (= becoming human), we identify with him through faith. Faith bonds us to Jesus.

The apostle Paul was therefore able to claim "*I have been crucified with Christ; and it is no longer I who live, but Christ lives in me; and the life which I now live in the flesh I live by faith in the Son of God, who loved me, and delivered himself up for me*" (Gal 2:20). Through faith in Christ, the genuine believer experiences mystical union with Christ and his crucifixion so that the believer has in effect suffered death with Christ as the justifying punishment for their sin. *This is the meaning of justification*: "for the one who dies has been justified from sin" (Rom 6:7).[4] Upon their death, the covenant violator is justified, they've suffered their just punishment, so that now liberated they are able to enter into a new covenant with God. The broken covenant has been remedied by the sacrifice required. Death, the wage of sin, has been paid.

God's forgiveness through Jesus' vicarious sacrifice accomplishes acquittal and reconciliation without the compromise of God's holiness or justice. And God's mysterious plan proves effective in solving the problem of sin. God overcomes evil with good through the sacrificial death of Jesus appropriated through faith.

Faith is thus more than an intellectual belief or a statement of intellectual assent. It is a vicarious identification with Jesus' crucifixion that is motivated by genuine confession of sin, a resolute turning away from sin, a wholehearted turning to God, and a genuine pledge of fidelity to the risen Christ as Lord. The individual's confessed guilt before God acknowledges that *their* sin, which *they* have committed, has separated them from God and made necessary their punishment in death. This coming to grips with the reality of sin and its consequences enables the true believer to identify with Jesus on the cross. As James Denny explained: "And this is what the Atonement means: it means the mediation of forgiveness through Christ,

---

4. Greek = "*ho gar apothanōn dedikaiōtai apo tēs hamartias*" (NA[27]).

and specifically through his death. Forgiveness, in the Christian sense of the term, is only realized as we believe in the Atonement: in other words, as we come to feel the cost at which alone the love of God could assert itself as Divine and holy love in the souls of sinful men."[5]

Thus faith has a vicarious dimension that sets the authentic believer apart from the nominal sports fan. As Christ identified with us in his becoming human (the incarnation), so too does God call upon the believer to identify with Christ vicariously through faith. This vicarious at-one-ment includes the cost of discipleship. It is not the product of a cheap grace or an uncostly sacrifice. It plumbs the depths of the human soul. *As we are not saved by a cheap grace, neither are we justified by a nominal faith.* This passionate vicarious identification lies at the very heart of one's saving union with Christ. It is an intellectual belief, yes, but even more so it is a committed relationship of passionate love expressed in genuine worship from the heart in spirit and truth.

But that is not all. God's plan does not end in death. Indeed, Paul explains further that not only do genuine believers identify with Jesus' death but also with his burial and resurrection. Such is the symbolic message of baptism:

> Or do you not know that all of us who have been baptized into Christ Jesus have been baptized into his death? Therefore we have been buried with him through baptism into death, in order that as Christ was raised from the dead through the glory of the Father, so we too might walk in newness of life. For if we have become united with him in the likeness of his death, certainly we shall be also in the likeness of his resurrection, knowing this, that our old self was crucified with him, that our body of sin might be done away with, that we should no longer be slaves to sin; for he who has died is freed from sin. Now if we have died with Christ, we believe that we shall also live with him, knowing that Christ, having been raised from the dead, is never to die again; death no longer is master over him. For the death that he died, he died to sin, once for all; but the life that he lives, he lives to God. Even so consider yourselves to be dead to sin, but alive to God in Christ Jesus (Rom 6:3–11).

Baptism thus symbolizes God's grace in action as he works through his re-creative power to punish, bury, and raise from the dead the one who has faith in Christ. Union with Christ results in eternity with God.

---

5. Denny, *Atonement and the Modern Mind*, 33.

But even that is not all. Atonement also means discipleship—a life of participation in the ministry of Jesus. Thus Jesus taught his followers that "if anyone wishes to come after me, let him deny himself, and take up his cross, and follow me" (Mark 8:34). In the same spirit, Paul cautioned, "For you it has been granted for Christ's sake, not only to believe in him, but also to suffer for his sake" (Phil 1:29). Atonement is permanent, so that the believer endorses Jesus' lifestyle and ministry. Against the background of Romans 6:1–13, atonement thus matures into Christ-like discipleship when the baptized believer participates in the very same ministry that once ministered to them.

Reconciliation

Faith in Christ involves active participation in the reconciling work of Jesus. Whereas the Humpty Dumpty crash had left all relationships in conflict, the new covenant work of Christ aims to reverse the consequences of sin through unifying reconciliation. Paul puts it simply: "For all of you who were baptized into Christ have clothed yourselves with Christ. There is neither Jew nor Greek, there is neither slave nor free man, there is neither male nor female; for you are all *one* in Christ Jesus" (Gal 3:27–28). This reconciliation is yet another accomplishment of the cross, which has put to death the enmity between former enemies amongst newly created sons of God (Eph 2:14–18). "Paul argues that Jews and Gentiles are united in sin, all being in Adam; similarly, they can be united in salvation, all being united with Christ and becoming one as children of Abraham, having faith in God and being credited with righteousness."[6] This call to participate in reconciliation is an active one. Passive disapproval of racism falls short of the biblical call. *Proactive* participation in reconciliation is the tenet of genuine Christian discipleship.

We Walk in the Footsteps of the Faith of Abraham

It is self-evident that this kind of salvation is impossible without genuine belief in God's power to make it happen. As we saw in chapter 3, Scripture reveals that God chose Abraham to be the recipient of his covenantal relationship on the basis of Abraham's faith that God could give him a

---

6. Marshall, *Aspects of the Atonement*, 131–32.

son through his barren wife Sarah. Abraham, in other words, believed that God could create life from nothing—the essential truth about God conveyed by Genesis 1. It is for this reason that the apostle Paul singles out Abraham as the biblical prototype for saving faith:

> For this reason it is by faith, that it might be in accordance with grace, in order that the promise may be certain to all the descendants, not only to those who are of the law, but also to those who are of the faith of Abraham, who is the father of us all, (as it is written, "A father of many nations have I made you") in the sight of him whom he believed, even God, *who gives life to the dead and calls into being that which does not exist.* (Rom 4:16–17)

Critical to Paul is the observation that God's choice of Abraham on the basis of his faith occurred before the giving of the law, before the building of the temple, and before the development of Israel's religion. And, we might add, even before the writing of the Bible. Salvation, Paul urges, is not a religious matter; it is a covenant—a relationship with God that God bestows upon those who genuinely believe in him as God and walk with him as Lord of their lives. As Hebrews 11:6 affirms: "without faith it is impossible to please him, for he who comes to God must believe that he is, and that he is a rewarder of those who seek him."

Paul's message is that God still chooses his covenant partners on the basis of faith: "'The word is near you, in your mouth and in your heart'— that is, the word of faith which we are preaching, that if you confess with your mouth Jesus as Lord, *and believe in your heart that God raised him from the dead,* you shall be saved; for with the heart man believes, resulting in righteousness, and with the mouth he confesses, resulting in salvation" (Rom 10:9–10). As Abraham believed that God could give life to Sarah's barren womb, so now the genuine believer is called upon to believe that God recreated life in Jesus' dead body. Both expressions of faith, Abraham's and the contemporary Christian's, require basic belief in God as creator of life. For if God created life in the beginning, simple logic affirms God's ability to create, recreate, and resurrect in the present and in the future. Both expressions of faith affirm that God desires relationship exclusively with covenant partners who believe in him as he really is—the creator and sustainer of life who genuinely does love us.

The Ethics of Vicarious Identification

The phenomenon of vicarious identification helps us to understand the radical depth of Jesus' standard for living. Just as vicarious union helps us to understand how the believer may experience crucifixion, burial, and resurrection with Christ, so also does vicarious union help us to understand the deceptive nature of sin. Lustful fantasy *stimulates* and then *simulates* sexual interplay with a person other than one's present or potential future covenant partner in marriage, so that Jesus was able to affirm: "everyone who looks on a woman to lust for her has committed adultery with her already in his heart" (Matt 5:28). Pornography is a covenant violation and an act of disobedience against God, who knows the heart and desires holiness and "truth in the innermost being" (Ps 51:6). God's standard for the covenant, we recall, is love with *all of* one's heart, soul, *mind,* and strength. Pornography is a mental act of defiance against God's design for marriage. Directly counter to the positive contours of vicarious identification with Christ through faith, pornography is a negative act of vicarious union with a prostitute (one selling their body for money). The one celebrates covenant, the other destroys it. The one consummates marriage, the other disregards it. The one is real; the other is a warped frustrated imitation. "Do you not know that the one who joins himself to a harlot is one body with her? For he says, 'the two will become one flesh.' But the one who joins himself to the Lord is one spirit with him" (1 Cor 6:16–17).

Using the rhetorical device of personification, James tracks a similar thought by applying personal attributes to lust in his depiction of sin: "But each one is tempted when he is carried away and enticed by his own lust. Then when lust has conceived, it gives birth to sin; and when sin is accomplished, it brings forth death" (Jas 1:15). In this extended metaphor, sinners engage sexually with their own lust. Lust then conceives like a pregnant whore and gives birth to sin. Sin then brings forth death. Sin is thus an evil parody of the atonement. At-one-ment with lust results in eternal death as at-one-ment with God results in eternal life. In rejecting relationship with God, the sinner lustfully chooses relationship with sin and suffers the consequence of death.[7]

---

7. Compare Isa 66:4: "So I will choose their punishments, and I will bring on them what they dread. Because I called, but no one answered; I spoke, but they did not listen. And they did evil in my sight, and chose that in which I did not delight."

In the same way, video games that simulate murder, rape, robbery, and prostitution are very real manifestations of sinful rebellion against God and lead insidiously to moral corruption. For in the playing of these games the participant vicariously identifies with the robber, the murderer, the rapist, and engages sexually with the prostitute—all in the spirit of entertainment. In the end, while union with Christ results in conformity to God's image (2 Cor 3:18; Gal 4:19; Phil 3:21), fanciful identification with sin results in the death of character. Each pilgrimage takes place within a person's innermost being.

The New Covenant: You may be Born Again

"How can a man be born when he is old? He cannot enter a second time into his mother's womb and be born, can he?" (John 3:4). Nicodemus's starkly literal question begs a resounding "no" answer. Of course one can't physically be born again! The very idea is absurd. And yet his question gets a resounding "yes" from the sweeping message of the Bible. A person may indeed be "born again" without physically reentering their mother's womb. As Jesus depicts in the "Parable of the Prodigal Son" (Luke 15:32),[8] so Paul asserts in his doctrinal argument in 2 Corinthians: "If any man is in Christ, he is a *new* creature; the old things passed away; behold, new things have come" (2 Cor 5:17). The Bible speaks of a spiritual resurrection that happens in the life of the believer prior to death and bodily resurrection. Paul's symbolic explanation of baptism is again instructive: "Even so consider yourselves to be dead to sin, but *alive to God in Christ Jesus*" (Rom 6:10–11). In Colossians 3:1, Paul similarly exhorts: "If then you have been raised up with Christ, keep seeking the things that are above, where Christ is, seated at the right hand of God."

God's solution to the problem of sin caused spiritual death is the new covenant whose features we charted in chapter 3. Jesus, Paul, and the author of Hebrews (8:6–13; 10:15–18) all identify the new covenant—new relationship with God as accomplished by Jesus' death and resurrection—as the goal of salvation.

Jesus, of course, is the Davidic Son of God prophesied in Isaiah 9:6–7, Jeremiah 33:14–16, and Ezekiel 37:24–27. He is the "anointed one," the Messiah who reverses the consequences of sin: he cleanses lepers, heals the blind, lame, deaf, and dumb, and raises the dead. Moreover, he

---

8. "for this your brother *was dead*, and is alive; he was lost, and is found."

attempts to re-gather God's people from exile, as Luke 13:34–35 makes plain. Jesus' miracles pronounce the arrival of the long hoped for day of salvation—the coming to pass of God's new covenant reconciliation with his former covenant partner. As Luke 7:22//Matthew 11:2–4 affirms, *Jesus* himself is the agent of God's transforming, healing work—"the blind receive sight, the lame walk, the lepers are cleansed, and the deaf hear, the dead are raised up, the poor have the gospel preached to them. And blessed is he who does not stumble *upon me.*"

Jesus voluntarily pursued the cross with the goal of salvation in mind, believing that his death would provide the blood of the new covenant. Thus in giving the elements of the Passover he affirmed, "This cup which is poured out for you is the *new covenant* in my blood" (Luke 22:20; cf. 1 Cor 11:25; Matt 26:28; Mark 14:24). What did this mean except that Jesus' death was going to activate and bring into effect the "new covenant" promises: the removal of idols, the anointing of the Spirit, the transformation of the heart from stone to flesh, and restoration from exile. As the ancient Hebrews had offered a sacrificial lamb on Passover to maintain covenant relationship with God, so now Jesus was offering himself as a sacrifice in the place of what would be the new covenant people of God.

Hosea strikingly envisions a day when God will forgive adulterous Israel by removing the names of the idols from her mouth (Hos 2:17) to betroth Israel to himself *forever* in righteousness, justice, loving-kindness, and compassion (Hos 2:19–20). As Paul proclaims later, the image is of total transformation: "I will call those who were not my people, 'my people,' and her who was not beloved, 'beloved.' And it shall be that in the place where it was said to them, 'you are not my people,' there they shall be called sons of the living God" (Rom 9:25–26). Hosea 6:1–2 affirms this as radical "born again," "conversion" theology: "Come let us return to the Lord. For he has torn us, but he will heal us; He has wounded us, but he will bandage us. He will *revive* us after two days; He will *raise us* up on the third day that we may *live* before him" (Hos 6:1–2).

The same awareness is ever present in Paul's letters, where he identifies himself as a "*servant* of the *new covenant*" (2 Cor 3:6). As such he is empowered by the Holy Spirit to reverse the hardening caused by idolatrous sin through the preaching of the gospel. "You are a letter of Christ," Paul says of the Corinthians, "cared for by us, written not with ink, but with the Spirit of the living God, not on tablets of stone, *but on tablets of human hearts*" (2 Cor 3:2–3). Echoes of Deuteronomy 30, Ezekiel 36, and Jeremiah 31 are unmistakable.

This, too, is the message of Romans 1–3, where Paul preaches God's gracious gift of Jesus' sacrifice (Rom 3:25) as the solution to the plight of idolatrous sinners, who, having worshiped the creature rather than the Creator, were given over by God to foolish, darkened hearts (Rom 1:21–25). Salvation from this state of hardened depravity requires God's forgiveness and human transformation. Paul explains that God's rescue of sinners accomplishes just that—for "the love of God has been poured out *within our hearts* through the Holy Spirit who was given to us" (Rom 5:5). This is "new covenant," "born again" salvation made possible only by God's re-creative power.

Hence, where sin once abounded in suffering and death, God's grace now hyper-abounds in forgiveness, resurrection, and reconciliation in a new covenant—a new relationship between the loving creator and the repentant forgiven believer. God, having reckoned the believer one with Christ through faith, not only reckons the believer crucified but also *raised* with Christ to no longer suffer the residual hardening effects of sin. The believer is born again *not* into the likeness of his or her former self, but into the likeness of Christ, so that God considers the born again person fully obedient and fully faithful, *just like Jesus*. They are now mystically *in* Christ, *with* Christ, and *in the body of* Christ. In this newly created state the believer is able to live not just in peace with God, but in a relationship of intimate *sonship* with him, so that one is able to pray to God as to *Abba Father*, just as Jesus did: "For all who are being led by the Spirit of God, these are the sons of God. For you have not received a spirit of slavery leading to fear again, but you have received a spirit of adoption as sons by which we cry out, 'Abba! Father!' The Spirit himself bears witness with our spirit that we are children of God" (Rom 8:15; see also Gal 4:6; Mark 14:36). And so it is that Paul testifies, "It is no longer I who live, but *Christ* who lives in me" (Gal 2:20a). The restored new covenant is thus a relationship—not mere mutual acceptance but the intimate love of *sonship* as God intended it in the beginning. Jesus thus taught his disciples to pray, "Our Father . . ." (Matt 6:9).

Inseparable from this saving work is God's creation of what we now call the church. Being in Christ and with Christ through the power of faith, the believer becomes a member of the corporate body of Christ, the church. As I was both Lou Brock and a St. Louis Cardinal, so the believer in Christ identifies with Christ individually and corporately. As the covenant was originally with Abraham but also for the entire people of God, so it is with Christian salvation—believers die with Christ individually through faith, but raise to newness of life within the newly created corporate people of God. Membership in the body of Christ, the church, is thus the newfound identity of all beneficiaries of the new covenant work of Christ. To be a Christian is to be a member of the church.

This new covenant imagery serves as the conceptual background to Paul's theology in Romans 9, where Paul builds upon the new covenant visions of Hosea 2:23; 1:10, and Isaiah 10:22. Paul conceives that the promises given Hosea and Isaiah have now been ushered in through the death and resurrection of Jesus the Davidic Messiah (Rom 1:1–3) for the transformation of a new people: "I will call those who were not my people, 'my people,' and her who was not beloved, 'beloved.' And it shall be in the place where it was said to them, 'you are not my people,' there they shall be called sons of the living God" (Rom 9:25–26). Hosea 6:1–2 clarifies that Paul envisions a corporate outcome from new covenant "born again," "conversion" theology: "Come let us return to the Lord. For he has torn *us*, but he will heal *us*; he has wounded *us*, but he will bandage *us*. He will revive *us* after two days; he will raise *us* up on the third day that *we* may live before him."

Following the new covenant promise of Isaiah 1:9, Paul reaffirms in Romans 9 that God will save a remnant. This remnant, however, will not be a random, arbitrary choice on God's part. The remnant will be constituted of those who have exercised explicit faith in Christ: "just as it is written, 'behold, I lay in Zion a stone of stumbling and a rock of offense, and he who *believes* in him will not be disappointed'" (Rom 9:33 based on Isa 28:16; 8:14). The church therefore represents the remnant of human beings who have genuinely believed in Jesus as Lord. Paul's theology is thus fully consonant with John 3:16—that "whosoever believeth in him shall not perish but have eternal life."

Recreation in the Image of God

Salvation in the end thus involves God's action to restore his original design for humanity. Originally, "God created man in his own image" (Gen 1:27). Then Adam and Eve sinned, bringing upon all humanity ever since the incurable, terminal "cancer" that separated humanity from God and corrupted God's image in man. Then God acted to reestablish relationship with humanity through his covenant with Abraham. This covenant was originally given to Abraham and his descendants, but was then made available to all nations through the ministry of Jesus Christ. This relationship, Paul explained, was evidence of God's gracious love and was given exclusively to those who believe, as Abraham did, in God's ability to give life to that which does not have life, finding its ultimate expression in God's resurrection of Jesus Christ (Rom 4:24; 10:9–10). Through faith the believer vicariously identifies with Jesus' death, burial, and resurrection, so that they are born again into newness of life with Jesus and the reconstituted people of God.

Paul explains that God's work in Jesus is thus a reversal of the consequences of Adam's sin and a glorification of God's original design for humankind:

> For if by the transgression of the one, death reigned through the one, much more those who receive the abundance of grace and of the gift of righteousness will reign in life through the one, Jesus Christ. So then as through one transgression there resulted condemnation to all men, even so through one act of righteousness there resulted justification of life to all men. For as through the one man's disobedience the many were made sinners, even so through the obedience of the one the many will be made righteous. (Rom 5:17–19)

> For as in Adam all die, so also in Christ all shall be made alive. (1 Cor 15:22)

> So also is the resurrection of the dead. It is sown a perishable body, it is raised an imperishable body; it is sown in dishonor, it is raised in glory; it is sown in weakness, it is raised in power; it is sown a natural body, it is raised a spiritual body. If there is a natural body, there is also a spiritual body. So also it is written, "the first man, Adam, became a living soul." The last Adam became a life-giving spirit. (1 Cor 15:42–45)

Paul's anticipation of this event helped inspire the celebrative chorus of 1 Corinthians 2:9: "Things which eye has not seen and ear has not heard, and which have not entered the heart of man, all that God has prepared for those who love him."

In this newfound state of being, the believer discovers a new reality. They have become Christians—that is, they are anointed by the Holy Spirit as Christ was (the word *Christian* means *anointed one-like* = *Christ-like*). The love of God having been poured out within the believer's heart through the Holy Spirit who was given to them (Rom 5:5), the believer begins the process of re-conforming to the image of God: "But we all, with unveiled face beholding as in a mirror the glory of the Lord, *are being transformed into the same image* from glory to glory, just as from the Lord, the Spirit" (2 Cor 3:18). Rebirth is followed by growth, transformation, and recreation in the likeness of Jesus. This was the goal of Paul's discipleship as he informed the Galatians: "My children, with whom I am again in labor until Christ is formed in you" (Gal 4:19).

However, the growth process does not consummate in this lifetime, as Jesus' ministry did not terminate with his death. The final restoration of the image of God in humanity takes place after the believer's physical resurrection from the dead: "For our citizenship is in heaven, from which also we eagerly wait for a savior, the Lord Jesus Christ; *who will transform the body of our humble state into conformity with the body of his glory,* by the exertion of the power that he has even to subject all things to himself" (Phil 3:20–21). It will thus be God's creative power working through Christ that will accomplish the final act of salvation—the recreation of his faithful people back into his divine image.

The apostle Paul represents all true Christianity with the explicit charge that the resurrection is to be taken literally as a physical and spiritual change:

> And just as we have borne the image of the earthly, we shall also bear the image of the heavenly. Now I say this, friends, that flesh and blood cannot inherit the kingdom of God; nor does the perishable inherit the imperishable. Behold, I tell you a mystery; we shall not all sleep, but we shall all be changed, in a moment in the twinkling of an eye, at the last trumpet; for the trumpet will sound, and the dead will be raised imperishable, and we shall be changed. (1 Cor 15:49–52)

Christ the Victor

Ironically, the cross also brings the anti-god to justice: "Since then the children share in flesh and blood, he himself likewise also partook of the same, that through death he might render powerless him who had the power of death, that is, the devil" (Heb 2:14; see also John 16:11; Rev 12:11). The cross is God's chosen instrument both for salvation *and* for punitive judgment. This dual function comes forth clearly in Jesus' pronouncement in John 12:31–32: "Now judgment is upon this world; now the ruler of this world shall be cast out. And I, if I be lifted up from the earth, will draw all men to myself." Salvation sounds the defeat of Satan.

This feature of salvation is an already/not yet phenomenon. On the one hand, Satan is defeated on the cross where Jesus accomplished the climactic event of history that ensured the victory of God and the final success of God's original plan for creation. Since then Satan's insidious efforts have been forever defeated.

But he is not yet dead. Still to come is Satan's final demise as the Book of Revelation discloses: "And the devil who deceived them was thrown into the lake of fire and brimstone, where the beast and the false prophet are also; and they will be tormented day and night forever and ever" (Rev 20:10). Thus will conclude the story of evil and all perpetrators thereof.

Satan is not God's evil equal. And no one else is either. Certain destruction is the end for all who consider equality with God something to be grasped. Stemming from God's absolute knowledge of all that has happened, absolute justice will be the end of evil (Rev 20:12–13). Those who do not die with Christ in faith will die apart from Christ in judgment.

Why Jesus is the Only Way

While the Bible is explicit in revealing that Jesus is the only way to salvation (John 14:6; Acts 4:12; 1 Tim 2:5–6; 1 John 5:12), our postmodern world finds the exclusiveness of Christianity disturbing. Isn't it arrogant and unfair?

The salvation we have discussed is unfair only if we disregard the crucifixion of Jesus and the active love of God revealed in the gospel. When listeners understand the message of the cross, it becomes apparent that the exclusive way to God through Jesus is beyond fair, for it is rooted in the humiliating, tortuous self-sacrifice of Jesus who died in total innocence as the Son of God to satisfy the justice of God in payment for sin. The message of salvation through Jesus is a message of *mercy* and *grace* for all, though effective only for those who receive the benefits of Jesus' death through faith. In reality, Jesus is the only way for at least six reasons:

1. Eternal life and resurrection require the works of re-creation that Christianity alone promises. To unite with Christ is to unite with

the creator, which alone makes a born again, new creation salvation possible. Neighboring faiths have no counterpart to this dimension of Christianity.

2. Neighboring faiths that require good works for salvation fall short of providing a solution to the inherent problem of sin. As a person with a terminal cancer will not find healing from exercise and a better diet, so a person with sin will not recover through the Band-Aid of good works. New covenant salvation offers an inner healing (Ezek 36:22–36) that is foreign to neighboring faiths.

3. Christianity is unique in its offer of atonement with God through faith enabled union with Jesus' death and resurrection. Neighboring faiths require the denial or dismissal of sin without justice being done. Christianity uniquely explains how a sinner can experience punishment for their sin and come out on the other side as fully just, clear of conscience, and fit for eternal life with a sinless God.

4. Christianity is alone true to reality in its awareness that forgiveness alone makes peace possible both with God and with other human beings. Because of the reality of evil, pacifism simply doesn't work. Because of the human appetite for revenge, retributive justice only incites further conflict. War may silence conflict, but it escalates hatred in the long term. Only grace exercised through sacrificial love and forgiveness works. Such is the peace of Jesus (John 14:27).

5. Jesus alone makes possible atonement with sinless, holy God, because of all human beings Jesus is the only one to have ever lived a sinless life (Heb 5:8–10). Union with any other martyr would not have the same saving effect because all other unions would be with sinners just like us. Jesus alone, as the writer of Hebrews emphasizes, was tempted as we are and yet without sin—thereby becoming a uniquely perfect sacrifice (Heb 4:15). As the saying goes, "he became like us that we might become like him." Prophets of neighboring faiths fall short of Jesus in that they were not God incarnate and they were all sinners. To become more like them would be to become more like the sinners we already are.

6. Jesus is the only way because God has appointed him Lord and judge (Phil 2:5–11). Jesus' judgment will be based on how human beings relate to his truth: "And I say to you, everyone who confesses me

before men, the Son of Man shall confess him also before the angels of God; but he who denies me before men shall be denied before the angels of God" (Luke 12:8–9; see Matt 10:33). To reject Jesus is to reject God: "he who rejects me rejects the one who sent me" (Luke 10:16). To deny Jesus is to deny God: "Whoever denies the Son does not have the Father; the one who confesses the Son has the Father also" (1 John 2:23). Jesus is thus unlike prophets of neighboring faiths, because he is Lord (Phil 2:5–11). He is the only one of his kind (John 1:14, 18).

Conclusion

Biblical theology attests that what is impossible with human beings is possible with God. One *can* be born again. In coming to Jesus one comes to the living Word of God who created life in the beginning and who wills to recreate life in those who place their faith in him. The essential question, therefore, is not resurrection but creation *ex nihilo* (= out of nothing).[9] For if Genesis 1:1 and John 1:1 are true, the resurrection is entirely plausible—if God really does love us. For if God created life in the beginning, and if he continues to love his chief creation, whom he's created in his own image, then it is entirely reasonable to think that God can and will act in his creative power to *recreate* his loved ones who have perished. That this *is* reality is the essence of the gospel of Jesus Christ: "God so loved the world that whoever believes in him will not perish but have everlasting life."

And prior to God's work of bodily re-creation, which is what resurrection is, one may be born again through God's present transforming work in the heart of the believer through the regenerating power of the Holy Spirit. This new covenant work of Christ removes idols, ushers in the Holy Spirit, transforms the inner being, and writes the law of God upon the heart (Heb 8:7–12), so that the death destined sinner becomes a new creation with a new destiny. The gospel is that sovereign God wills that this rebirth happen in the lives of those who believe in him and love him as their Lord and God.

9. For a thorough defense of creation *ex nihilo* see Copon and Craig, *Creation out of Nothing*.

Salvation is an extension of creation theology that works itself out in all of Scripture including the Pauline doctrine of the righteousness of God. German New Testament scholar Peter Stuhlmacher expresses this well: "Only when one follows this perspective and sees that God causes his righteousness, *which creates salvation,* to be effective for Jews and Gentiles, that is, for all humanity, in the sending, death, resurrection, and lordship of Christ, does the gospel of the righteousness of God which the apostle preaches take on a real worldwide dimension as well as taking on a relevance from the perspective of the theology of creation."[10]

The solution to sin is thus God's creative work through the covenant, which he has brought to perfection through the ministry of Jesus. Salvation is a creation from the mind of God.

In conclusion, the Bible's answer to Nicodemus's famous question is a resounding "no." God is not the God of the absurd—To be "born again" does not mean physical reentrance into the mother's womb to be born, live, and die again. Rather, something much, much greater is in view. The believer is born again into union with the resurrected Christ to share in Jesus' inheritance of eternal at-one-ment with the true, living God (John 17:20–21). To be "born again," to experience true conversion, is to experience the very believable transformation that God the creator *ex nihilo* wills to accomplish in the lives of those who confess Jesus as Lord and believe in their hearts that God raised him from the dead. This belief, if authentic, expresses itself in deeds of Christ-like sacrificial love made possible by the indwelling of the Holy Spirit (Rom 5:5).

New covenant conversion happens when God himself breathes new life into the spiritually dead sinner thereby bringing about a totally new creation. This transformation begins now as Paul explains in 2 Corinthians 3:18, but does not consummate until the future, as Paul further explains in Philippians 3:21. Much more than an intellectual discovery, a religious experience, or a form of philosophical enlightenment, conversion is a real *relational* union with the true, living, existing re-creating God. This union restores the image of God to the believer, which was God's original design (Gen 1:27). The revelation of this truth comes by way of Scripture—the wisdom that leads to salvation through faith in Christ Jesus.

10. Stuhlmacher, *Paul's Letter to the Romans,* 32. Italics added for emphasis.

Questions for Discussion, Further Study, and Meditation

- Why did Jesus have to die in order to forgive sin?
- How is it possible and just for God to forgive sins that people commit against other people and apparently not directly against God?
- In your own words, define the biblical concept of atonement.
- How does the atonement relate both to the individual's salvation and also to the corporate salvation of the church?
- Why is faith an essential requirement for salvation?
- How does the covenant concept relate to salvation?
- In what ways is salvation both a present reality and a promise not yet fulfilled?
- In light of the fact that no physical violation takes place, what's wrong with pornography and violent video games?
- How would you respond to atheist H. L. Mencken's comment that "Religion was invented by man just as agriculture and the wheel were invented by man, and there is absolutely nothing in it to justify the belief that its inventors had the aid of higher powers, whether on this earth or elsewhere . . . What the faithful Christian professes to believe, if put into the form of an affidavit, would be such shocking nonsense that even bishops and archbishops would laugh at it."[11]

Suggested Scripture Reading

Exodus, Deuteronomy 6–8, 30; Isaiah 11, 25, 40, 42, 50, 53, 61; Daniel 7; Ezekiel 37; Mark 8, 10, 14–15, John, Romans 3–8; 1 Corinthians 15; Revelation 20–22

---

11. Mencken, *Treatise on the Gods*, x–xi.

5

The Self-Authenticating Power of Scripture

Creation, sin, covenant, and salvation all entered reality before the canonization of the Bible. Truth isn't true because the Bible says it's so. Biblical truth is true because the Bible accurately represents preexisting reality. Scripture is God's tool for revealing the essential components of truth that human beings need to understand in order to live in peace with God and with one another. Scripture doesn't create truth; it reveals truth.

According to Scripture, God himself is the beginning and end of comprehensive truth. He is the "Alpha and the Omega, the beginning and the end" (Rev 21:6). According to Scripture, Jesus, God incarnate, is the way, the truth, and the life (John 14:6). He is risen from the dead as the authoritative Lord who empowers Christian discipleship and evangelism (Matt 28:18–20). God's exclusive design for new creation, the forgiveness of sins, atonement within the new covenant, and eternal salvation happens through actual encounter with the risen Christ followed by confession, repentance, and persevering faith in Christ crucified and risen from the dead. God is on his throne right now and human history is unfolding in tragedy and triumph in direct correlation with humankind's rejection or adoration of God himself.

The Bible is God's written instrument for communicating these truths to the humanity he created and loves. The Bible is not God, of course, but it is God's inspired revelation of essential truth in matters that relate to humanity's eternal relationship with God. From it, in a unique way, one may gain "the wisdom that leads to salvation through faith which is in Christ Jesus" (2 Tim 3:15). Or as John puts it, "these things have been written in order that you might believe that Jesus is the Christ, the Son of God; and that believing you may have life in his name" (John 20:31). Through Scripture we come to understand how God desires reconciliation and continued relationship. He has solved the problem of sin, overcome evil with good, and is inviting sinners to reunite with him through faith in Christ. One can be born again.

Written by prophets and apostles who were inspired and commissioned by God with unique authority, the Bible is the exclusive written standard for authentic Christian faith. Orthodox Christianity thus rejects as false all beliefs and practices that deviate from God's revealed word.

Upon conversion, many Christians discover that they have a sudden hunger to read the Bible. Why is this?

The question takes us back to the covenant. We recall from chapter 3 that kingship and marriage are the Bible's premiere metaphors for covenant relationship with God. God is king. Members of the covenant are his people. God is husband. The church is his bride.

As in all healthy relationships, covenant partners grow closer to one another through communication and learning about one another on deeper and deeper levels with the passage of time. Likewise, one who experiences atonement with God enters a relationship where the desire to know God becomes acute. In this relational process, revelation in nature, prayer, the indwelling of the Holy Spirit and meditation in Scripture are God's designed means for communication and self-revelation. Lived out both corporately and privately the life of theological meditation becomes a living act of worship where one discovers the truth that people do not in fact live by bread alone. The covenant member hungers for God's word and finds it uniquely satisfying and inspirational as a stimulus toward abundant life.

Yet, outside of covenant intimacy, "because the Bible says so!" is not a persuasive argument to unbelievers in the contemporary world. And it's easy to understand why. If someone is not yet persuaded of God's existence or his love, they're hardly going to believe in the authority of what they don't presently believe to be God's word. For people such as this the Bible is not yet authoritative, and they are not predisposed to believing that it tells the entire truth. "Because the Bible says so," smacks of dogmatism—the infamous refuge of the lazy mind.

This audience usually finds modern criticisms of the Bible convincing, not necessarily because of the substance of the criticisms made against the Bible, but because they presuppose the trustworthiness of erudite credentialed scholars at prestigious institutions who espouse disbelief. How could scholars like celebrated UNC Chapel Hill Professor Bart Ehrman, who draws attention to *human* elements in Scripture that act to undermine confidence in the supernatural origin of the Bible, be wrong?[1] How could outspoken atheist Richard Dawkins be wrong in his scathing attack on the God of the Hebrew Scriptures? How could this best selling Oxford don be wrong in his confident assurance that this is exactly the kind of world one would expect if there were no God, no good, no evil, and no intelligence behind creation?

Obviously, skeptics observe, the Bible was written by human authors with human vocabularies and human biases toward God and everything else. Therefore what we have in the Bible is not God's revelation of truth but a human religious invention—and an ancient, outdated one at that. Some biblical events here and there may have really happened, but the supernatural elements—prophecies, healings, resurrections, direct acts of God, miracles—are all fictional creations of the ancient religious imagination. In this respect the Bible is like the sacred writings of other neighboring faiths: valuable for the study of religious history but essentially bogus in regard to real truth.

Presupposed, of course, is the posture that "scholarly" observation necessitates minimalism and cynicism. It is self-evident that the Bible is full of human errors and contradictions. One only has to look at the history of the Bible's being passed from one generation to the next to discover that some copies of the Bible have alterations and errors that other copies don't have. The existence of multiple variants and translations seems to undermine biblical authority. Clearly not all Bibles are the same, so how can we speak of one authoritative text?

Similarly, the skeptic is mindful of the fact that the Bible is not homogenous in its revelation. The Four Gospels—Matthew, Mark, Luke, and John—all have different portrayals of Jesus. Each, it is said, betrays its author's unique biases and interpretations. Furthermore, skeptics expose what they view as discord among the apostolic authors, who sometimes appear to contradict one another as in the apparent contradiction

1. Ehrman is particularly relevant to the college audience as the author of Oxford University Press's widely distributed college textbooks for the study of the New Testament.

between Paul's emphasis on justification by faith and James's emphasis on justification by works.[2] Such differences require that the Bible be considered not one book but rather a collection of many disparate books of independent origins. Therefore, considering its diversity, how can the Bible be said to be the coherent word of one God?

Can the Bible Stand on its Own?

To some degree contemporary, well-intentioned evangelicals have paved the way for these arguments to become weightier than they really are. Prioritization of one biblical label or another has become the distinguishing litmus test for authentic Christianity even among many evangelical intellectuals. Anyone who does not sign a pledge of allegiance to the preferred technical term often suffers suspicion, distrust, and even pejorative labeling. The resulting impression is that evangelical Christianity can be exceedingly narrow—when evangelical scholars exclude other evangelical scholars from scholarly "Christian" fellowship on the basis of exclusive extra-biblical technical terms. To the skeptic, it goes without saying that this closed approach to scholarship lacks the integrity of the academic freedom that the broader academic world offers. A closed society, it is thought, must have something to hide and perhaps also something to fear. Here I am referring of course to the Evangelical Theological Society in America where written allegiance to the following statement of inerrancy is a requirement for membership: "The Bible alone, and the Bible in its entirety, is the Word of God written and is therefore inerrant in the autographs."

Is an extrabiblical technical term an appropriate criterion for excluding believers from fellowship—under any circumstances? Should a pledge of allegiance to a classification for the Bible really be a necessary requirement for inclusion into Christian fellowship? If it is for the most informed, credentialed evangelical scholars, then one would think that it should also be for all who claim to be authentic Christians.

But such is clearly not the case in evangelical churches around the world where membership in the body of Christ is based on faith in Jesus

---

2. Properly understood, Paul and James share the understanding that genuine faith is displayed through a Christ-like lifestyle. Paul takes works seriously (Rom 2:6), while James' emphasis is that works are outer evidence of genuine inner faith (Jas 2:14–26)—that faith without works *isn't faith at all.*

as Lord and God's saving action through Jesus' death and resurrection. Here there seems to be a disconnect between the church and the evangelical academic community. Why is the church at large more inclusive than the evangelical scholarly community?

Is the requirement of allegiance to contemporary technical terms biblical? What would Jesus think—or Paul? For each repeatedly reinforced the truthfulness of the gospel through appeal to the content and inherent authority of Scripture, but never did they appeal to a party slogan or a theological technical term.

Recourse to Scripture itself may prove instructive. In his letter to the Galatians, Paul vehemently argued to the earliest churches that external markers such as circumcision and legalistic observation of holy days were unnecessary for Christian fellowship, even though Christian legalists were requiring them as a prerequisite for inclusion among the covenant people of God (Gal 4:8–11). Boldly, Paul attacked this false teaching going so far as to rebuke the apostle Peter, when Peter's exclusion of Gentiles on the basis of food laws contradicted his earlier inclusion of all peoples on the basis of faith alone (Gal 2:11–16).

Jesus argued similarly in the Gospels—"This people honor me with their lips, but their heart is far away from me. But in vain do they worship me, teaching as doctrines the precepts of men" (Matt 15:8–9; Isa 29:13). Knowing Jesus' elevation of the love of God and the love of neighbor as the highest commandments, it's hard to accept a pledge to a technical term as a valid biblical criterion for excluding others from a worshiping community. What is an exclusive technical term but a "precept of men"? And why stand behind an extrabiblical precept, when one can bank one's hopes directly on *Sola Scriptura*, the word of God alone?

According to the Bible itself, what matters most to God with respect to the new covenant is not an external statement of assent, but an internal heart of true covenant devotion to the true living God who raised Jesus from the dead (Rom 2:28–29). True Christianity is not proven by an external written pledge but by a transformed heart. The vitality of the Christian faith is deeper, stronger, more robust, and more intentionally unifying than lip service to a creedal statement or a password into a private society. And identification of God's true people is God's prerogative, not humankind's.

By giving the impression that the point of departure for biblical authority is a technical term or phrase, ironically, zealous defenders of the

Bible may preempt the Bible's own entry point to the wisdom that leads to salvation through faith in Jesus Christ. The place to begin is Genesis 1. The place to end is Revelation 22. Why add requirements and encumbrances to God's word? If the Bible needed a protective amulet, one would think that God would have added one himself. Since he didn't, why not be biblically conservative and conserve Scripture as it is? The Bible stands secure on its own.

While skeptics may not respond to "because the Bible says so," they often do respond to actual encounters with the living God. This is how it has always been. It's instructive to observe in this respect that before the writing of the Bible, the impetus for Abraham's faith was an encounter with the true living God. Prior to the writing of the New Testament, the impetus for the faith of the disciples and the earliest Christian church was direct encounter with the resurrected Jesus. Prior to the letters he wrote, the impetus for Paul's conversion was a personal encounter with the risen Lord Jesus on the road to Damascus. And the canon closes with the Book of Revelation disclosing a series of visions that the risen Jesus revealed through angels to the apostle John on the island of Patmos. Revelation's authority derives not from its human classification as part of the canon, but from its apostolic origin as an eyewitness description of God's action in history.

Christians should therefore be careful to not subordinate theology to bibliology when in fact the Bible itself has it the other way around. Encounter with God himself became the subject of Scripture with respect to creation, God's reaction to sin, God's creation of the covenant, and God's work of salvation through the historical ministry of Jesus. God is the authority and object of faith upon whom Christians base their salvation and eternal security, and it is the present indwelling of the Holy Spirit that is our authenticating pledge of salvation and eternal wellbeing. That the Bible reveals these truths as the word of God written is a self-authenticating reality for those who have encountered God and experienced the transformation of their lives through Jesus' saving ministry and the continued indwelling of the Holy Spirit. What the biblical writers wrote was true to their experiences with God and that truth remains true to reality now for those whose encounters with God are followed by repentance, confession, and a lifetime of obedient, active faith carried out in the life of the body of Christ. The walk of faith is not motivated by blind allegiance to a human construct but is motivated by an ongoing covenantal relationship with God through genuine atonement with him. And it is here that the Bible exercises supernatural power as the word of God, the sword of the Spirit. For the Bible fully complements the work of the Holy Spirit in transforming minds as God conforms believers to his own image (Rom 12:1– 2; Phil 3:20; 2 Cor 3:18). Marriage with God matures and deepens through genuine engagement with Scripture.

Yes, God in his mysterious wisdom speaks through Scripture today, both through direct encounter in private meditation and through the preaching of his word. This contemporary reality, as testified to by millions of genuine Christians, accords fully with the testimonies of the earliest followers of Jesus. Paul's letter to the Galatians attempted to restore this basic awareness: "You foolish Galatians, who has bewitched you, before whose eyes Jesus Christ was publicly portrayed as crucified? This is the only thing I want to find out from you: did you receive the Spirit by the works of the law, or by hearing with faith?" (Gal 3:1–2). Paul reminds us that the earliest Christians received the Spirit of God through hearing the gospel preached. And so it is today. *Biblical* preaching still gives the wisdom that leads to salvation through faith in Christ Jesus. Such is the power of Scripture as an instrument of God. As Paul affirms of the OT, "these things . . . were written for our instruction" (1 Cor 10:11).

What is essential to reality is that the Bible is a self-authenticating and trustworthy expression of God's divine revelation that truthfully guides God's people to wisdom and salvation. The truth of God is revealed in Scripture.

What Does the Bible itself Say?

The Bible reminds us that we shouldn't be surprised at the confusion of contemporary conflicts over the Bible and other sacred subjects—*all* are sinners and have fallen short of the glory of God. That *all* includes the wordsmiths of the Evangelical Theological Society statement on inerrancy, self-promoting skeptics like Bart Ehrman and Richard Dawkins, every Christian that attends church on a given Sunday, authors of pop theology, and the author of this book. Ironically, conflict evidences the truth of Scripture both within and without the religious community. Because of the Fall, ours is a Humpty Dumpty world and unity doesn't come instinctively.

In the face of this divisive reality, Scripture aims to unify believers in the body of Christ. If we persevere in studying Scripture and devote ourselves to living according to its teaching, we shall inevitably become more like one another as we become more like God. Being prone toward self-promoting isolationism, we need the Bible as an objective benchmark to pull us back to unadulterated truth. According to the Bible itself, the goal of Scripture is not exclusivism but evangelism (John 20:30–31; 2 Tim 3:14–16), and the goal of spiritual maturity is not exclusivism but unity in the body of Christ (John 17:22–23; Phil 1:27; 2:1–2).

In that spirit it is a corrective to observe that the Bible does *not* identify itself as the way, the truth, and the life or as the authority that originally commissioned the apostles and the church. In fact, knowledge of the Bible is not the intended goal of the Bible. The purpose of the Bible is to reveal knowledge that leads to Christ—"true knowledge of God's mystery, that is, Christ himself, in whom are hidden all the treasures of wisdom and knowledge" (Col 2:2–3). According to the Bible, Jesus is "the way, the truth, and the life" and the exclusive way of salvation (John 14:6). Jesus is the authority who commissioned the early church (Matt 28:18–20) and is today the ultimate source of all wisdom and knowledge (Col 2:2–3).

These observations do not lessen the importance of Scripture but act positively to put the Bible in proper perspective. Scripture is God's written invitation to a life of wisdom and salvation in Christ.

At the same time, the Bible is explicit in revealing that God intended for the Bible to be written by human beings with human vocabularies, human minds, and human personalities. The authors of the Old Testament and New Testament were human beings. The prophets wrote to their own generations. Luke wrote to a man named Theophilus. Paul wrote to *people* who were in Rome, Corinth, Philippi, and Galatia. *Of course the Bible is human in orientation.* And the reasons are simple and true to life. The biblical authors communicated the message of God to real human beings in their own languages in terms they could understand. God apparently did not intend the Bible to be interpreted as a divine book written in an angelic language devoid of human contribution. The human authors of Scripture all wrote the consistent and coherent truth that God inspired them to convey to their different audiences. Their vocabularies and writing styles were therefore distinctive and different. Each tailored their messages to the learning capacities of their readers in order to communicate effectively. *Of course the Bible is human in orientation.* And it makes perfect sense that the Bible's humanness accords with God's will. To establish an atoning relationship with human beings, God chose to communicate in human languages.

Diversity does not preclude the Bible from being inspired by one God. According to 2 Timothy 3:16–17, God inspired this collection of human writings in order for it to become *Scripture*; that is, to communicate his design for humanity and his plan for salvation—to give the wisdom that leads to salvation in Christ. Nowhere does the Bible present itself as promising to be copied perfectly from one generation to the next or that it was to be devoid of human orientation in every respect. Clearly, if such was the case, the Bible has failed, because the only Bibles that exist today do have variant readings and do have the interpretive contributions of their human authors, editors, and translators.

But the Bible has not failed in its intent. Generation after Christian generation has testified to the power of Scripture in leading intelligent human beings to the saving grace of God, which God exercised through the ministry of Jesus. Such have been the history-changing testimonies of Augustine, Luther, Wesley, and Barth, whose worldviews and very lives were transformed permanently by the divine revelation found in Paul's letter to the Romans.

I may humbly add that my own reading of Scripture has consistently substantiated the real life truthfulness of 2 Timothy 3:16–17. God has worked through Scripture by his Holy Spirit to guide me to truth, to wisdom, and to the deep realities of salvation. The Bible has disciplined me, corrected me, and kept me accountable to God's standards of ethics, love, and moral responsibility. As my foremost accountability partner, the Bible has protected me from rationalization and pride—the recreation of God in my own mental image. The Bible has served effectively as my canon (= Gk. for *measurement* or *standard* for faith and practice). When I have failed, the Holy Spirit has convicted me with the aid of the Bible to lead me to confession, repentance, and the joy of forgiveness. The reading of the Bible has cultivated my life of worship and the intimacy of my relationship with God. In these practical ways reminiscent of 2 Timothy 3:16, the Bible has worked in this world of reality in my own personal life. And the certainty of this reality is beyond dispute in my mind and well beyond the misguided missiles of atheistic skepticism and the acids of uncontrolled higher critical methodologies.

Variant readings and human interpretations fall far short of disproving the Bible's divine inspiration. Who can say that God didn't inspire John's identification of Jesus with the Word, which "was with God in the beginning" (John 1:1–3)? Couldn't God inspire an interpretation just as easily as he could the original events? Why not? Who conceived this rule that cynical scholars live by? Are the cynics entirely trustworthy agents of factual truth? Or are their degrees and reputations all that matter? Isn't appeal to authority without supporting evidence a classic logical fallacy? Why not question the questions of those who question the Bible—especially when millions of testimonies throughout history have authenticated the Bible's truth claims?

Yes, of course, cynics are right that we do not have an inerrant original copy of any of the biblical texts. But how significant is that? If God exists, and if our reality accords with his plan, then the Bible we have is the Bible that God always intended—not a hypothetical Bible that presently does not exist. That means that our Bible, with all of its human scribal errors,[3] variant readings, and dissimilar translations is adequate for God's intended purpose, which is the communication of his love for humanity and his message of salvation made possible through Jesus' death and resurrection. *It is the content that matters.*

The Bible is inerrant in its revelation of the truths of creation, covenant, sin, and salvation. These truths are inexorable axioms, supernatural laws that order life in the real world where forgiveness really does work. Prayer works. Sacrificial, responsible love works. Confession and repentance work. Sin and its consequences are real and have obvious adverse consequences. The Holy Spirit is alive and active. Jesus' death and resurrection do make atonement with God possible. The church is doing the work of the risen Christ in the world today.

A slippery slope from scribal error to heresy or from scribal error to untrustworthiness is a paranoia Christians need not have. What is there to fear in biblical criticism? The Bible, as it really is, can stand on its own in withstanding intellectual assaults. The Bible has never been considered

---

3. We should be careful to guard against exaggerating the destructive force of the phenomenon of scribal errors and variants. The vast majority of scribal errors in the critical apparatus of the Hebrew Scriptures and the Greek NT are insignificant *erratica* comparable to modern editorial oversights that are easily explained and have little to no impact on the substance of the text. The few larger variants do not create inner thematic contradictions that would compromise biblical theology.

sacred because of its language—common Hebrew, Aramaic, and Greek—or because of an avowed freedom from human error. The Bible is sacred and holy because it reveals the truth about God's identity and his action in creation, his establishing relationship with his people, his exercising love in revelation, discipline, and prophecy, and his action to save a people that he loves and desires to have eternal relationship with through the atoning work of Christ's death and resurrection. The real truth of this message has never been disproven, nor can it be. And it is not endangered at all by contemporary scholarship—whether competent or pseudo.

Thus, a pledge of allegiance to the Bible or to a technical classification for the Bible is not essential—perhaps for an exclusive society but not for relationship with God. As in the cases of Abraham and Paul, intellectually honest human beings today will not believe the message of the Bible until they have had an actual encounter with the true living God. And even then they may not come to salvation, unless they willfully enter an obedient covenant relationship with God on his terms. Like the majority who originally heard the warnings of Moses, the prophets, John the Baptist, Jesus, and Paul, people today must respond in repentance, confession, and persevering obedient faith in order to know true intimacy in an eternal relationship with God. According to the Bible, they may hear his voice but turn away out of a preference for the gods of their own making. And so it is that the Bible advises: "Today, if you hear his voice, do not harden your heart" (Heb 3:7–8, 15; 4:7).

In the end what matters most is the truthfulness of what the Bible says. Does God exist in this world as a personal relational being? Does God still speak through nature, his Holy Spirit, and through Scripture according to his revealed purposes? Does God, the creator of the heavens and the earth, still sustain natural life and the entirety of this universe? Is our present predicament the result of sin? Does sin really cause problems that still plague the human race? Is sin against God really the reason for suffering, death, and continued confusion? Does God really love this world? Does God still have the power to recreate, to resurrect? Is God still active in meeting people where they are today? Does God still desire love, fidelity, and intimate relationship? Does the Bible still reveal the character of God *as he really is*? Would it really be good to be holy as God is holy? What would the world be like if people everywhere kept the Ten Commandments—not out of legalism but out of *agape* love? Does forgiveness work in real life today? Is there really inherent meaning and purpose in life, or is the reality that we know the mere consequence of physical cause and effect?

Contemporary skeptics cannot deny that all of these questions can be answered affirmatively with plausible logic, if Christian testimonies like mine are true and God really is the one whom the Bible claims him to be. Skeptics base conclusions on an absence of evidence within their own experience whereas believers base their conclusions on the presence of evidence within theirs. The former is no more intellectual than the latter. Arguably, cynics can only offer presuppositions that are equally or more faith-based than the building blocks of Christianity—that is, that our reality is the mere result of a spectacularly unlikely coincidence that happened millions and millions of years ago when unthinking nonliving substances slowly became spectacularly complex intelligent living cells— a miracle thus far impossible of duplication and impossible of persuasive explanation. The critical thinker has to decide—*are miracles without God more believable than miracles with him?* I find the latter far more persuasive.

Mysteries, of course, exist. The Bible doesn't explain everything, nor is the explanation of everything its intention—"God's ways are not our ways, his thoughts are not our thoughts" (Isa 55:8–9). We "view through a glass dimly" (1 Cor 13:12). "Oh, the depth of the riches both of the wisdom and knowledge of God! How unsearchable are his judgments and unfathomable his ways!" (Rom 11:33). There is much we do not understand.

However, for those who know God, God's existence makes coherent sense of day to day living reality. True love and true joy are realities that transcend the natural world. Redemptive love is every bit as real as destructive evil. The indwelling of the Holy Spirit is an experienced reality that the authentic people of God share with past generations of intelligent believers of intellectual honesty and integrity. Sin does have consequences and there is a universal awareness of absolute justice. Forgiveness works. Without it no relationship lasts, because in truth all human beings are sinners who need frequent forgiveness. In truth we are like grass that withers and passes away. Death is a reality, but so too is creation! If science requires an analogy, we have it in the created world that surrounds us. What God created in the beginning, he can recreate. Christian hope bases itself on this coherent, intelligent faith.

Why Some People Just Don't Get It

If the Bible does make sense, and the evidence of God's action in history and in the lives of his people is so evident, why then are there so many intelligent people who reject faith? Why don't they get it?

Several years ago while I was still in my early forties, my eyes suddenly opened to a reality I'd never fully appreciated—trees. Though my eyes had seen them all my life, I'd never really *seen* trees with eyes that saw their diversity, the detail of their leaf patterns, the design and color of their bark, the shape of their crowns, and the color, pattern, and smells of their wood. I'd walked through woods all my life without really *seeing* trees for what they really are.

Then a few years back, after an unplanned, extended submersion in the forest, my eyes began to gradually open. Whereas before I had seen big trees and little trees, hardwoods and evergreens, now I began to see endless variety in focused detail: Persimmon, Redbud, Hackberry, Sassafras, Black Locust, Beech, Hawthorne, Pawpaw, Pignut Hickory, Black Walnut, Sycamore, Sugar Maple, Black Gum, Ohio Buckeye, Blue Ash, Wild Black Cherry, Bur Oak, White Oak, Red Oak, Chinkapin Oak, Cottonwood, Shagbark Hickory and on and on—all thriving in central Indiana.

The potential for sight was with me all along, dormant and locked, waiting to come forth with vital passion and invigoration. Though I still don't see everything that a forester does, I now have sight to see all kinds of things that I didn't see before. Sight has proven to be an unexpected source of inspiration and pleasure, a genuine enhancement of my life, and a more accurate understanding of a beautiful part of reality.

One of my favorite friends is an octogenarian named Marian Townsend. Like mine, Marian's eyes have been opened to the spectacular realities of the forest. But Marian's sight extends much further. Marian has a passion not only for trees, but also for wildflowers, mushrooms, birds, mammals, astronomy, Indian lore, and history (not to mention, of course, our other common interest—the Bible). Marian's eyes are so open in fact that those close to her refuse to let her drive for fear that she might swerve off the road while watching something of interest out the driver's side window. Marian's dangerously interested in lots of things.

Though dangerous, Marian gets it. Her eyes are open to see things that most people can't. Yet her world is not imaginary. It's more real than the business mentality that fixates on the bottom line. Her world is more alive, more wonderful, and more true to comprehensive reality.

Similarly, the truth and reality of the gospel can only be appreciated by those who have eyes to see its reality and truth. Like folks who can only see trees as natural resources for building materials, for fuel, or for economic profit (all good things) and therefore are forever unable to appreciate the priceless beauty of the forest, so also readers of the Bible can become so engrossed in extraneous theories, methods, arguments, philosophies, denominational conflicts, and theological debates that they become disabled and even blinded from seeing the Bible's real message. Or, having bought into the erudite disbelief of a popular cynic, they foreclose the door to God without giving him a second thought. They won't even consider going into the forest and taking a look around. These don't discover the Bible to be inspiring, because they've never really been in the Bible with ears to hear the inspired word of God. They've been in something else that has a motive other than the revelation of wisdom that leads to salvation in Christ Jesus. Cynically distrustful of ultimate wisdom from the start, they fail to see it even though they may read it in the original language with apparent ease. They can read through the Bible without perceiving a thing. They have eyes but they can't see.

The Bible explains that spiritual blindness relates directly to the human preference for securities of our own making as opposed to the security of God's kingship: "Hear this, O foolish and senseless people, who have eyes, but see not; who have ears but hear not. Do you not fear me? Declares the Lord. Do you not tremble in my presence?" (Jer 5:21–22). God's message to Jeremiah was that his contemporaries were so preoccupied with idols that they had become numb to God's existence, though his power was as evident as the sea. They had eyes but they could not see.

Jesus' parable of the "Sower and the Soils" makes the same point (Mark 4:1–25). In this parable Jesus compares people to different kinds of dirt—some are like ground beside a road, others like rocky soil, still others are like thorny soil, and finally some are like fertile ground. The ones who are like the thorny soil are "the ones who have heard the word, and the worries of the world, and the deceitfulness of riches, and the desires for other things enter in and choke the word, and it becomes unfruitful" (Mark 4:18–19). Those like the thorny soil don't really desire God because their infatuations and fixations are on the here and now. They have no time for God. They are blinded by the distractions of earthly securities. If things are good, they don't perceive their need for God. If things are bad, they think relief can only come from a this-worldly solution. They have eyes with the potential to see the reality of God all around them, but anxious striving for bigger and better in the here and now has blinded them from the only eternal security that really matters.

Ironically, the self-sufficient intellect's rejection of the gospel is exactly what the Bible anticipates: "For the message of the cross is foolishness to those who are perishing, but to us who are being saved it is the power of God . . . The man without the Spirit does not accept the things that come from the Spirit of God, for they are foolishness to him, and he cannot understand them, because they are spiritually discerned" (1 Cor 1:18; 2:14; NIV). In isolation the intellect is inadequate, because God is bigger than the human mind.

My eyes opened to the reality of trees through extended submersion beneath a forest canopy near my home. In separation from the internet, cell phones, television, and all human contact, I walked for hours until a realization became a passionate awareness. Creation is vital. Exploring it and tending it is a pleasure that is refreshing, therapeutic, and exhilarating. Hidden life and worlds of fascination are everywhere, even today in our polluted world.

What I discovered in the forest is waiting to be discovered in every dimension of life—physics, mathematics, chemistry, biology, literature, music, theatre, history, astronomy—and most of all in deeper truer relationships with God and those around us. Wisdom, understanding, and abundant life are waiting to be had—they're crying out to be had.

Similarly, spiritual blindness is healed only through submersion in the presence of God. One must say yes to God to know him. For only through baptism in the Holy Spirit of God does the Bible come alive with the power of understanding. Distractions, anxieties, and temporal securities aside, God's eternal salvation will only be found by those who seek him with all their heart by entering and persevering in a covenantal relationship of faith: "if my people who are called by my name humble themselves and pray, and seek my face and turn from their wicked ways, then I will hear from heaven, will forgive their sins, and will heal their land" (2 Chr 7:14); "you will seek the Lord your God, and you will find him if you search for him with all your heart and all your soul" (Deut 4:29).

God's salvation involves a relationship that endures earthly anxiety and doubt through persevering commitment—in many ways just like human relationships. Patience, mercy, forgiveness, grace, communication, thought, commitment, faithfulness, devotion, and genuine responsible love are all necessary in intimacy with God as in all relationships. Relationships don't result from intellectual syllogisms or formal ceremonies or technical buzz words. They result from commitment, desire for permanent devotion, and a being together in confident trust. Similarly, salvation is a comprehensive persevering relationship—uniquely exhilarating at times and devoted always.

In other ways, however, God's relationship with his people is unlike human relationships. Relationship with God is unique because God is God and we are not. The covenant we speak of is therefore not a parity covenant between two equal parties, but a suzerainty covenant between mortal human beings and the immortal God of absolute power. The posture of relationship is thus not one of shoulder to shoulder diplomacy or negotiation, but a posture of worship, of reverence, and awe. God is a "consuming fire" (Heb 12:29), whose presence evokes wonder and exhilaration but also awe and respect. "There is an infinite gap in worth and dignity between God the Creator and man the creature, even though man has been created in the image of God. The fear of God is a heartfelt recognition of this gap—not a put-down of man, but an exaltation of God."[4]

The salvation that Jesus accomplished is thus a new covenant relationship of constant communion between this awesome faithful God and his newly created, faithful people. Remarkably, to use the Bible's own metaphor, salvation is a marriage. God's infinite love makes him willing and his awesome power makes him able—to forgive, purify, sustain, and resurrect those who believe in him and love him with all their heart, soul, mind, and strength.

As Scripture, the Bible thus reveals this wisdom that leads to salvation in Christ. It is a salvation that surpasses human calculation—"things which eyes has not seen and ear has not heard, and which have not entered the heart of man, all that God has prepared for those who love him" (1 Cor 2:9). Like other dormant passions that lie before us waiting to be unlocked, the inspiration of Scripture eagerly awaits exploration by the repentant child of God.

It may be that a large part of heaven will involve the opening of our senses to realities that have always been before us, but which we haven't

---

4. Bridges, *Practice of Godliness*, 27.

had activated faculties to detect. We will see that the evidence for God was always overwhelmingly present in all of creation and within our own bodies. We will discover that we were surrounded by the miraculous every day of our mortal lives. We will then wake up to see, hear, and comprehend all that God has prepared for those who love him. In this spirit, having been awakened to the reality of God, C. S. Lewis advised, "Look for Christ and you will find Him and with Him everything else thrown in."[5] Such is indeed the prophecy of Scripture:

> And I saw a new heaven and a new earth; for the first heaven and the first earth passed away, and there is no longer any sea. And I saw the holy city, new Jerusalem, coming down out of heaven from God, made ready as a bride adorned for her husband. And I heard a loud voice from the throne, saying, "Behold, the tabernacle of God is among men, and he shall dwell among them, and they shall be his people, and God himself shall be among them, and he shall wipe away every tear from their eyes; and there shall no longer be any death; there shall no longer be any mourning, or crying, or pain; the first things have passed away." And he who sits on the throne said, "Behold I am making all things new." And he said, "write, for these words are faithful and true." (Rev 21:1–5)

The purpose of the Bible is to reveal God as God really is. Theological precision enabled by Scripture is essential because human beings have a selfish tendency to resist God as he really is and to conform God to the image of human philosophies, theologies, political systems, gender biases, and even ethnic prejudices. In the face of this fallen human tendency, the Bible stands steadfast as an objective benchmark declaring God's holy and transcendent nature. His ways are not our ways and his will is that we not conform to the comforts of our prejudices but transform into his likeness by the renewing of our minds (Rom 12:1–2; 2 Cor 3:18; Phil 3:20). Conformity to God's image reverses the consequences of sin and reestablishes God's original design, the image of God in humankind that was lost in Eden. The Bible works to this end in conjunction with the indwelling of the Holy Spirit. And in reality, Scripture does accomplish this purpose in the lives of those who submit to its instruction in faith and obedience.

The Bible, however, is not a juggernaut that requires intellectual suicide. Christians are free to explore and critique the Bible for all its worth in both its original languages and in its many translations. Following

5. Lewis, *Mere Christianity*, 190.

centuries of rational criticism, the Bible still stands as secure as ever. It accurately explains the origin of life as God willed to reveal it; it accurately explains the origin and continued effects of sin and evil; it accurately reveals the character of God and what it takes to enter and maintain covenant relationship with God through faith in Jesus Christ; it accurately reveals the meaning and power of salvation; and it prophetically forecasts how God will consummate this world with the resurrection of the dead, a final judgment, and a recreation of the heavens and the earth. Along the way the Bible reveals its own intended purpose (2 Tim 3:15–17). With respect to these all important intended revelations of Scripture, the Bible is the exclusive canon of God's written word—the authoritative written measure of God's authentic revelation. In *this* sense, the Bible is inerrant and entirely trustworthy for the purposes for which God breathed it into existence.

The deficiency of higher critical skeptics and atheistic scientists is not that they have thought too much, but that they have thought too little. In reaching foreclosure on God prematurely, they have sold themselves short on the comprehensive truth of all reality. For reality extends beyond the reach of the scientific method. Undirected materialistic coincidence cannot explain the phenomena of the conscience, sacrificial love, universal standards of ethics, and the human capacity for compassion. Discovery of these higher truths is the reward not only of believing Bible scholars and believing scientists but also of all believers whose faith heightens with cognitive discovery of God on an ongoing basis. There is neither foreclosure nor closure to the knowledge of God. His grandeur transcends the mind.

Questions for Discussion, Further Study, and Meditation

- In your own words, define the purpose of the Bible.

- What would be lost if Christians did not have the Bible?

- If the Bible is true, how do we explain the disbelief of many very intelligent Bible scholars?

- What is the relationship that exists between prayer, Bible study, the work of the Holy Spirit, and corporate worship in the life of the church?

- In what sense is the Bible the word of God written?

- What is the purpose of the biblical laws, if they are not intended to be a means for acquiring righteousness before God?

- Is it troubling to you that the canon of the New Testament was not closed until centuries after the death of Christ, and that its closure was not culminated by a direct mandate from God but by early church consensus? Why or why not?

- Do you agree with this chapter's reservations about using descriptions of the Bible as litmus tests for authentic faith? Why or why not?

- With respect to orthodox faith and practice, Roman Catholics consider church tradition, the Magisterium of the church, and papal decree to be equal with Scripture in authority. Is the Roman Catholic stance compelling? Why or why not?

- In your opinion, is the following argument of Mark Twain valid? "There is no evidence that there is to be a Heaven hereafter. If we should find, somewhere, an ancient book in which a dozen unknown men professed to tell all about a blooming and beautiful tropical paradise secreted in an inaccessible valley in the center of the eternal icebergs which constitute the Antarctic continent—not claiming that they had seen it themselves, but had acquired an intimate knowledge of it through a revelation from God—no Geographical Society in the earth would take any stock in that book; yet that book would be quite as authentic, quite as trustworthy, quite as valuable evidence as is the Bible. The Bible is just like it."[6]

6. Twain, "Reflections on Religion," 48.

Suggested Scripture Reading

Genesis 1; Psalm 119; Matthew 4:1–11; John 1:1; Romans 1:2; 15:3–4;
1 Corinthians 10:11; Galatians 3:8; 1 Thessalonians 2:13; 2 Timothy 3:14–
17; Hebrews 1, 4:12–13; 2 Peter 1:20–21; 3:15–16.

Bibliography

Alcorn, Randy. *Heaven.* Wheaton: Tyndale, 2004.

Anderson, Bernhard W. *Contours of Old Testament Theology.* Minneapolis: Fortress, 1998.

Anselm. *The Complete Philosophical and Theological Treatises of Anselm of Canterbury.* Translated by Jasper Hopkins and Herbert Richardson. Minneapolis: Banning, 2000.

Augustine. *On Free Choice of the Will.* Indianapolis: Bobbs-Merrill, 1964.

Bauckham, Richard. *The Climax of Prophecy.* Edinburgh: T. & T. Clark, 1993.

Bridges, Jerry. *The Practice of Godliness.* Colorado Springs: NavPress, 1983.

Clines, David J. A. *The Theme of the Pentateuch.* JSOT Supplement Series 10. Sheffield: Sheffield Academic, 1978.

Collins, Francis. *The Language of God: A Scientist Presents Evidence for God.* New York: Free, 2006.

Conway, David. *The Rediscovery of Wisdom: From Here to Antiquity in Quest of Sophia.* London: Macmillan, 2000.

Copon, Paul, and William Lane Craig. *Creation Out of Nothing: A Biblical, Philosophical, and Scientific Exploration.* Grand Rapids: Baker, 2004.

Craig, William Lane, and J. P. Moreland. *Philosophical Foundations for a Christian Worldview.* Downers Grove: InterVarsity, 2002.

Davies, Paul. "The Origin of Life II: How did it Begin?" No pages. Online: http://aca .mq.edu.au/PaulDavies/publications/papers/OriginsOfLife_II.pdf.

Dawkins, Richard. "God's Utility Function." *Scientific American* (Nov 1995) 85.

Denny, James. *The Atonement and the Modern Mind.* London: Hodder and Stoughton, 1903.

Doblmeier, Martin, director. *The Power of Forgiveness.* Journey Films, 2007.

Drummond, Henry. *The Greatest Thing in the World.* Springdale, PA: Whitaker House, 1981.

Ehrman, Bart. *God's Problem.* San Francisco: HarperOne, 2008.

Facione, Peter A. *Critical Thinking: A Statement of Expert Consensus for Purposes of Educational Assessment and* Instruction. Millbrae, CA: California Academic, 1990.

Flew, Antony. *There Is a God: How the World's Most Notorious Atheist Changed His Mind.* San Francisco: HarperOne, 2007.

Fowler, Thomas B., and Daniel Kuebler. *The Evolution Controversy: A Survey of Competing Theories.* Grand Rapids: Baker, 225.

Gilkey, Langdon. *Maker of Heaven and Earth: A History of the Christian Doctrine of Creation.* New York: Doubleday, 1959.

Hopkins, Gerard Manley. *God's Grandeur*. In *The Norton Anthology of Poetry*. Edited by Jon Stallworthy. 3rd ed. New York: Norton, 1983.

Ingersoll, Robert G. "The Gods." In *The Works of Robert G. Ingersoll*. 12 Volumes. New York: Dresden, 1900.

Lewis, C. S. *George MacDonald: An Anthology*. New York: Macmillan, 1947.

———. *Mere Christianity*. New York: MacMillan, 1952.

Marshall, I. Howard. *Aspects of the Atonement*. London: Paternoster, 2007.

Marshall, Paul. *Heaven is Not My Home: Learning to Live in God's Creations*. Nashville: Word, 1998.

Meadors, Edward P. *Idolatry and the Hardening of the Heart: A Study in Biblical Theology*. London: T. & T. Clark, 2006.

Mencken, Henry Louis. *Treatise on the Gods*. Baltimore: The Johns Hopkins University Press, 1997.

Mendenhall, George. "Covenant." In *ABD* 1:1179–1202.

Meyer, Stephen C. *Signature in the Cell: DNA and the Evidence for Intelligent Design*. San Francisco: HarperOne, 2009.

Mill, John Stuart. *On Liberty*. Harmondsworth, UK: Penguin, 1974.

Monod, Jacques. *Chance and Necessity: An Essay on the Natural Philosophy of Modern Biology*. New York: Knopf, 1971.

Peacocke, Arthur. *Evolution: The Disguised Friend of Faith?* Conshohocken, PA: Templeton Foundation, 2004.

Plantinga, Alvin. *God, Freedom, and Evil*. Grand Rapids: Eerdmans, 1977.

Plantinga, Cornelius. *Engaging God's World*. Grand Rapids: Eerdmans, 2002.

Rendtorff, Rolf. *The Covenant Formula: An Exegetical and Theological Investigation*. Edinburgh: T. & T. Clark, 1998.

Sagan, Carl. ABC *Nightline with Ted Koppel*, December 4, 1996.

———. *Cosmos*. New York: Random House, 1980.

———. *The Demon Haunted World: Science as a Candle in the Dark*. New York: Random House, 1995.

Shawcross, John T., ed. *The Complete Poetry of John Milton*. New York: Doubleday, 1971.

Sthulmacher, Peter. *Paul's Letter to the Romans*. Translated by Scott J. Hafemann. Louisville, KY: Westminster John Knox, 1994.

Swinburne, Richard. *The Existence of God*. Oxford: Clarendon, 1979.

———. "The Justification of Theism." No pages. Online: http://www.leaderu.com/truth/3truth09.html.

Tournier, Paul. *Reflections*. New York: Harper & Row, 1976.

Twain, Mark. "Reflections on Religion." In *The Outrageous Mark Twain*. Edited by Charles Neider. New York: Doubleday, 1987.

Webb, Stephen H. *The Dome of Eden: A New Solution to the Problem of Creation and Evolution*. Eugene, OR: Cascade, 2010.

Williamson, Paul R. "Covenant." In *DOTP* 139–55.

Yancey, Philip. Preface to *Orthodoxy*, by G. K. Chesterton. Colorado Springs: Shaw, 2001.